Camping Arizona

Camping Arizona

A Comprehensive Guide to Public Tent and RV Campgrounds

Third Editon

Bruce Grubbs

FALCONGUIDES

GUILFORD, CONNECTICUT
HELENA, MONTANA

AN IMPRINT OF ROWMAN & LITTLEFIELD

FALCONGUIDES®

Copyright © 2005, 2013 by Rowman & Littlefield
A previous edition was published by Falcon Publishing in 1999.

FalconGuides is an imprint of Rowman & Littlefield.
Falcon, FalconGuides, and Outfit Your Mind are registered trademarks of Rowman & Littlefield.

All photos by Bruce Grubbs
Maps by Bruce Grubbs © Rowman & Littlefield

Distributed by NATIONAL BOOK NETWORK

Library of Congress Cataloging-in-Publication Data
Grubbs, Bruce (Bruce O.)
Camping Arizona / Bruce Grubbs. — 2nd ed.
p. cm. — (A Falcon guide)
ISBN-13: 0978-0-7627-3413-9
ISBN-10: 0-7627-3413-2
1. Camp sites, facilities, etc.—Arizona—Directories. I. Title. II. Series.

 GV191.42.A7G88 2005
 917.91"068—dc22

                                         2004060758

ISBN 978-0-7627-8175-1

Printed in the United States of America

Contents

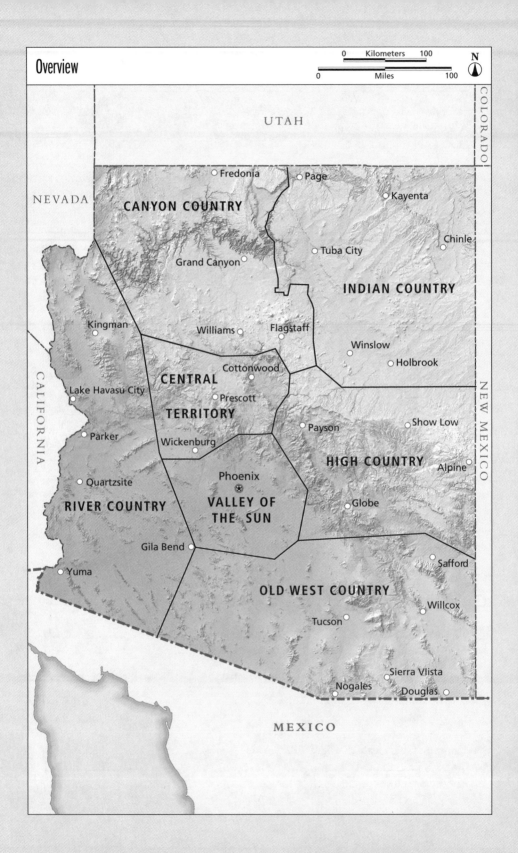

Kilometers 100

Miles 100

N

UTAH

COLORADO

NEVADA

CANYON COUNTRY

Fredonia

Page

Kayenta

Chinle

Tuba City

Grand Canyon

INDIAN COUNTRY

Kingman

Williams

Flagstaff

Winslow

Holbrook

Cottonwood

CENTRAL

CALIFORNIA

Lake Havasu City

Prescott

TERRITORY

Payson

Show Low

Parker

Wickenburg

HIGH COUNTRY

Alpine

NEW MEXICO

Quartzsite

Phoenix

VALLEY OF
THE SUN

Globe

RIVER COUNTRY

Gila Bend

Yuma

Safford

OLD WEST COUNTRY

Willcox

Tucson

Sierra Vlista

Nogales

Douglas

MEXICO

Acknowledgments

I have to credit my parents for starting me on a lifelong love of the outdoors by taking me camping at an early age. I also wish to thank my friends who over the years have shared many camps with me. Warm thanks to Duart Martin who backed this project gracefully. Special thanks to Jean Rukkila for reading the manuscript; she not only found errors but also added personal comments on some of the campgrounds. I greatly appreciate all the agency personnel who took the time to answer my queries, and then reviewed my descriptions of their campgrounds for accuracy. You are too numerous to mention, but this book would not have been possible without you. Special thanks to my editor Julie Marsh and all the fine people at Globe Pequot Press/FalconGuides who helped me update the second edition into this revised third edition.

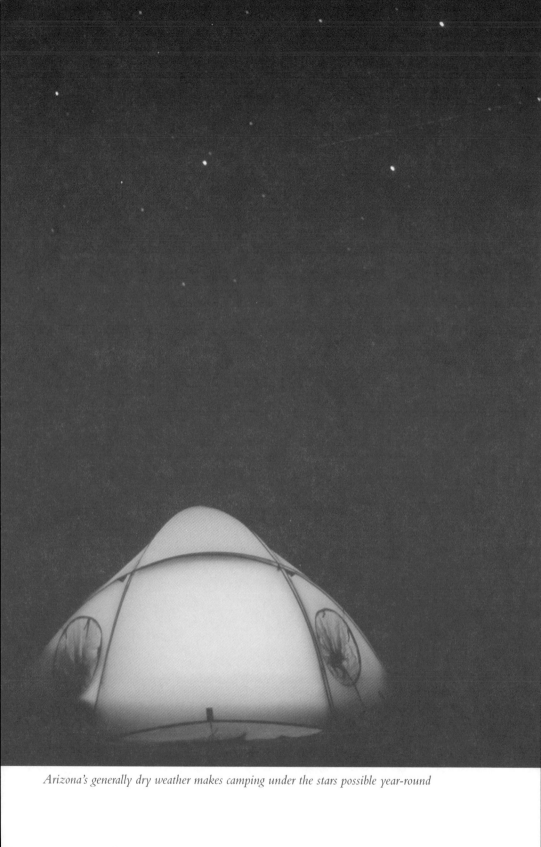

Arizona's generally dry weather makes camping under the stars possible year-round

How to Use This Guide

If you're looking for a concise, easy-to-use guide to the public campgrounds in Arizona, this is your book. This Falcon Guide is divided into seven major geographic divisions, each of which has its own unique characteristics—deserts, mountains, lakes, etc. Within the divisions, campgrounds are covered by areas. Each area has a map showing the campground locations, a quick reference table showing the campground facilities, and a description of each campground in the area. Photos of each area help you visualize the type of country you'll be camping in.

Use the Arizona Geographic Divisions map at the front of the book to choose the type of area appropriate to the season and your preferences, and then use the map of that particular division to pick the area you'd like to camp in. Refer to the quick reference table and descriptions to get information on a specific campground and compare it to others. Finally, use the campground map to locate the campground. Or you can riffle through the book until a photo catches your eye and then look for campgrounds in that area.

This book covers Arizona public campgrounds with developed sites that are accessible by vehicle. Reservation-only group campgrounds are not included, but if group camping is available in or near public campgrounds, it is mentioned in the campground description. Backcountry hike-in campgrounds, informal campsites, and campgrounds without developed sites are not included. Neither are the numerous private campgrounds and RV parks found in the state. (For private campgrounds, I recommend *Woodall's Campground Directory for North America,* revised annually.)

Organization of This Guide

The campgrounds in this book are divided into sections for each of the seven major geographic divisions of the state developed by the Arizona Office of Tourism. Each division has a map showing the general area and a general description of the division. Most of the divisions are further divided into regions based on a city or town within the region. Each region has a map that shows the locations of all the campgrounds covered in that region. There is also a description of the region, its recreational opportunities, and the nature of the camping in that part of the state. A list of contact addresses, phone numbers, and websites for getting additional information is also included.

Next there is a campground chart that summarizes the facilities at each campground in an easy-to-read format. Items listed include the campground number and name; its elevation; season of use; availability of RV and trailer sites; the total number of sites; the availability of drinking water, an RV dump (sanitary disposal station), fishing, hiking trails, boating, and boat launch; wheelchair accessibility; whether there is a fee; and the stay limit. Toilet facilities are not mentioned, since all the campgrounds included in this book have restroom facilities of some type. Please note that tent camping is available at all campgrounds listed in this book.

The campground number is keyed to the regional map and the detailed campground description. The campgrounds are more or less listed starting at the northwest corner of each region and then proceeding east and south across the region. There are a few exceptions to this order, mainly when terrain and campground access make it reasonable to change the order. Official agency campground names are used, but some maps and publications may show different or incorrect names.

The elevation of the campground, shown in feet, is useful for determining the climate and best season for camping. Campgrounds below about 4,000 feet are generally hot in summer but pleasant in winter. Campgrounds above approximately 7,000 feet are usually snowbound in winter and cool in summer. The season is the official agency season that the campground is open. Not all facilities may be available during the open season.

The RV/trailer column is checked if RV and/or trailer sites are available. If this column is blank, only tent camping is available in the campground. The sites column lists the total number of sites, which may be divided between tent and RV/trailer sites. Drinking water is not available in all campgrounds. If it is, the water column is checked. The water system may be turned off in cold weather or during the off-season, even though the campground is open. If a sanitary disposal station is available at the campground or nearby, the RV dump column is checked. In some cases a separate fee may be charged for this service.

If either lake or stream fishing is available at or near the campground, the fishing column is checked. Of course, the type and quality of fishing varies with the season and other conditions; check with the local Arizona Game and Fish Department office for more information.

A check in the hiking trails column means that nature and/or hiking trails are available at or near the campground. A nature trail is an interpretive trail with signs or a brochure that explains local nature features. Such trails are great for getting to know the local flora and fauna. Hiking trails are generally longer trails that can be used for day hikes and/or backpack trips. The boating column indicates whether boating is available at or near the campground. This may be either river or lake boating; the campground description will have detailed information. The boat launch column indicates whether a public boat ramp and launching facility is available. Wheelchair access, if checked, means that at least one campsite is wheelchair accessible.

A check in the fee column means that a fee is charged for each night's stay. The specific campground fee, if any, is not shown, since fees are subject to change. Campground fees generally vary with the amount and quality of the facilities provided, with more developed campgrounds charging more. Even different sites within the same campground may have different fees. Some campgrounds have very basic facilities and charge no fee. Finally, the stay limit (days) column shows the length of time you're allowed to camp at the site.

Campground Description

Campground descriptions follow the campground services chart and are listed in the same order as the chart. An at-a-glance section gives several items of information about the campground.

The **location** gives the campground's location in relation to the nearest town and appropriate natural features.

Sites gives the number of tent and RV sites, the maximum RV or trailer length, and the number of and type of hookups. If no maximum length is listed, the campground has no length restrictions.

Road conditions describes whether the access roads are paved, all-weather dirt, dirt, or a combination. Paved and all-weather roads are normally passable in all kinds of weather, but some roads may be closed for the winter season. Dirt roads vary greatly in their condition and degree of maintenance and are likely to become impassable in wet weather. Most dirt roads to campgrounds in this book are passable to ordinary vehicles in dry weather, if you drive with care. Exceptions are mentioned in the text.

Management gives the name of the agency or unit that manages the campground, along with a phone number and Internet address for obtaining current information. Many public campgrounds are now managed by private companies under contract. In some cases the contact number is for the private company.

Finding the campground provides directions to the campground from a nearby town. Usually this is the same town that the section is based on.

About the campground gives such information as nearby attractions, vegetation at the campground, the type of hiking trails, angling information, and the availability of group camping and showers.

Finally, the nearest services are described. "Limited services" means that the described town or location does not have all the services you would expect from a city, such as repair garages and large supermarkets. You can expect to find small gas stations with limited hours and small convenience markets in such places. "Full services" means that repair shops, supermarkets, and other city amenities are available.

Camping in Arizona

Arizona is a fascinating place in which to camp because of the state's variety of topography and ecosystems. You'll find high, forested plateaus, alpine mountains, deep canyons, and spacious deserts, as well as rivers, streams, and lakes.

Because of its large range of elevation, Arizona always has delightful weather somewhere, year-round. By picking your destination, you can enjoy perfect weather for your camping trip during any season.

During summer the low deserts in the central and southwest portions of the state are very hot. Temperatures often climb above 110°F and sometimes surpass 120° in the lowest, hottest locations. Camping in these conditions is enjoyable only by a lake or a river, where you can enjoy water sports. For that reason, most summer camping in the desert regions is done along the Colorado River and the reservoirs along the river and its tributaries in the central part of the state.

Most campers head for the mountains of southeast, central, northern, and eastern Arizona during summer. Here you can camp in the shade and majesty of the world's largest ponderosa pine forest. In July the hot, dry weather of early summer gives way to the North American Monsoon, when seasonal moisture moves into the state from the southeast and commonly triggers afternoon thunderstorms. Monsoon mornings in the mountains are usually clear and cool, but by late morning, cumulus clouds begin to fill the sky, often developing into thunderstorms by afternoon. The storms are usually brief, lasting an hour or so, but the rainfall may be intense and be accompanied by lightning and sometimes hail. After the rain showers stop, the mountain air is cool and sweet, and monsoon evenings are usually delightful.

During the autumn season, you can camp nearly anywhere in the state and enjoy good weather. The monsoon normally ends around mid-September as dry, cool air moves into the state. The mountains are still warm and pleasant during the day, although nights will be cold. As fall colors start to appear in the quaking aspen, Arizona sycamore, and other deciduous trees, the mountain forests take on their most striking appearance of the year. In the deserts the hot temperatures of summer moderate to merely warm, and the nights are cool.

In November the first winter storms signal the start of the winter wet season. These storms drop snow in the mountains and rain in the desert, but seldom last more than a couple of days. Between storms there is often a dry period of a week or more, and camping in the desert and mountain foothills up to about 5,000 feet elevation is usually very pleasant. Though winter nights in the desert can verge on cold, the warm southern sun makes the days pleasant and enjoyable. The mountains above 7,000 feet often have snow on the ground, and back roads are usually muddy or snowy and impassable. Nevertheless, a few campgrounds in the mountains stay open year-round to accommodate those who want a snow-camping experience.

Snowstorms are possible in the mountains as late as May, but usually the weather dries out in April. By mid-May most of the mountain high country is free of snow and the back roads are dry and passable. After wet winters, the desert country is a riot of wildflowers, starting as early as January in the lower desert areas and continuing into May in the higher deserts and grasslands. It's a show you don't want to miss. In spring, desert temperatures are still moderate and the mountains have warmed up, so you can camp nearly anywhere in the state.

Public Campgrounds

Public campgrounds in Arizona are run by several government agencies. Federal agencies include the National Park Service (NPS), the USDA Forest Service (USFS), and the Bureau of Land Management (BLM). The State of Arizona maintains a number of campgrounds through the state park system. In addition, several counties and cities operate public campgrounds.

The BLM has designated several Long Term Visitor Areas (LTVAs) in Arizona. These are special areas where camping is allowed for longer periods than the usual fourteen-day limit. LTVAs do not generally have developed facilities and are intended for self-contained RVs or trailers.

Group Camping Areas

Some campgrounds have special group areas; others are set aside for groups only. These areas usually require advance reservations. Call the managing agency well in advance to ensure getting your preferred dates.

Reservations

Some campgrounds accept reservations; others are first come, first served. Reservations can be made for many campgrounds by calling the National Recreation Reservation Service at (877) 444-6777 or online at recreation.gov. Otherwise, contact the managing agency at the number listed in the campground description.

Dispersed Camping

Dispersed camping—camping away from developed campground facilities—is permitted on some federal lands, primarily those administered by the USDA Forest Service and the BLM. There are large areas of the state, especially in the western deserts, where there are no developed campgrounds, so going out on your own is the only way to enjoy camping in these beautiful areas. The experience can be very rewarding, and it usually gets you away from the crowds.

Dispersed campers have special responsibilities. Certain areas such as designated recreation areas may be closed to dispersed camping. National parks and monuments and Arizona state parks do not usually allow dispersed camping. In areas that do allow dispersed camping, you'll have to be completely self-contained. It may be many miles to the nearest point of resupply. Since there is no trash disposal or site maintenance other than that provided by users, each camper must minimize his or her impact. Use the following guidelines to ensure that the next camper will find your campsite as good as or better than you found it.

- Cook on a camp stove—it's cleaner and more convenient than a campfire.
- Keep your campfire small.
- Use existing fire rings rather than building new ones.
- Pick up dead wood from the ground. Don't saw or chop on standing dead trees. Many species of wildlife depend on dead trees for homes.
- Don't burn trash. Most plastics give off toxic fumes when burned. Many food packages are lined with aluminum, which does not burn—it just melts into silvery blobs that remain forever.
- Don't bury trash. Animals will smell it and dig it up soon after you leave.
- Pick a tent site with natural drainage—on a slight slope or slightly domed patch of ground—so that you don't have to dig ditches.
- Don't drive or camp on meadows. Arid-land vegetation is fragile, and scars last many years.
- Carry and use a portable toilet, unless you're in a self-contained RV or trailer.
- If you have to answer the call of nature where there are no facilities, go well away from your campsite. Pick a spot at least 300 feet from open water and away from dry washes. Avoid dry, sandy areas if possible. Dig a small "cat hole" about 6 inches deep. Double-bag and carry out used toilet paper (baking soda helps control odor). When you're finished, re-cover the hole and restore the surface cover.

Camping with Kids

Why camp with your kids? There's a lot of good reasons. First of all, kids like to camp. I know I did when I was a kid. What may be a pretty ordinary campground to you is a world full of adventure to a child. If you can choose a campground with special appeal to your kids, so much the better. A kid who is interested in dinosaurs will be fascinated by fossil dinosaur tracks or a dinosaur quarry. Don't overlook kid attractions in nearby towns either. A trip to a hands-on science or natural history museum will make a camping trip memorable for kids, even though the trip takes you a few miles from your campsite.

Camping gets your kids into nature. If they grow up camping, they'll grow up being comfortable in the outdoors. They might even take up other outdoor sports on their own as they get older. And what's good for the kids is good for the whole family. Today's pace of life and the demands on us make it hard for families to spend time together. Camping naturally brings families together. Finally, camping is an inexpensive way for the family to vacation together. Even the most expensive campground is low cost compared to lodges and motels. You'll save even more money cooking your own camp meals. And if your kids are teenagers, it doesn't hurt to be away from malls and other shopping temptations.

Planning a camping trip with kids is a little different from planning a trip for adults. Because most kids naturally like camping, you have an advantage right from the beginning. Your challenge is to keep it interesting. Start by easing into camping. Take the kids on a few weekend outings before committing to a monthlong camping vacation. Find campgrounds near home to avoid long drives. Look for campgrounds that will be especially interesting to your kids. Make the trip comfortable for kids and adults.

In Arizona you have the luxury of picking the climate to camp in because of the great range of elevations in the state. Choose a campground where the weather will be pleasant—neither extremely cold at night nor excessively hot during the day. Also avoid camping where there are a lot of insects, such as mosquitoes. Generally bugs are only a problem in the mountains the first couple of weeks after snowmelt.

Remember your children's limited attention spans. Lounging around all day in a camp chair with a good book may be your idea of paradise, but your kids will get bored in about a minute. Include such physical activities as games or nature explorations. Let your kids help with camp chores. Because there are hazards in the outdoors that kids have to learn to recognize, you'll need to set rules that are different from those used at home.

What age is old enough to camp? That depends on you. Some parents take infants; others wait until the kids are in school. Younger kids might be more work for you, but you'll make a greater impression on younger kids. In Scandinavia kids are taken out on sleds by their cross-country skiing parents before they can walk. They learn to ski and walk at almost the same time. No wonder the Scandinavian countries produce so many winter sports Olympians!

Camping with your kids takes more effort, but your reward is the wonder of watching your kids discover nature and the outdoors.

Safety Precautions

While camping in Arizona is a very safe activity, a few precautions will ensure that your camping experience is an enjoyable one.

Fire Hazard

Fire danger is highest during late spring and early summer (May, June, and July) and early fall (October and November). When fire danger reaches extreme levels, wildfires start easily and spread explosively. Land managers may close certain areas to all public access during these periods. Don't be tempted to violate such fire closures. Not only are you risking your life if a fire should start nearby, you will very likely be cited and fined if caught in a closed area. Luckily, most fire seasons do not reach such extreme levels, although campfires are often restricted during June and July. Sometimes campfires are prohibited for dispersed campers but still allowed in official campgrounds. Occasionally campfires are prohibited everywhere. Please observe all campfire restrictions—for your own safety and to preserve the beauty of the forests and rangelands.

Smoking may also be prohibited on public lands during times of high fire danger. In extreme fire danger situations, smoking while traveling on foot or horseback may be prohibited in national forests. During these situations, USDA Forest Service regulations require that you stop and clear a 3-foot-diameter area down to mineral soil before smoking and that you extinguish all smoking materials before moving on. The Forest Service encourages you to do so year-round, because Arizona forests and grasslands can be dry any time of year. In addition, Arizona state law makes it illegal to throw burning materials, including cigarettes, from a moving vehicle. There are fire scars along most highways in Arizona that graphically show why these rules are necessary.

Weather

Hot weather is a serious hazard during summer months in the desert. Even in the mountains, the intense sun and extremely dry air can lead to heat-related injuries such as heat exhaustion and sunstroke.

Water is precious and scarce in the desert, and even the mountains are not as well watered as you might expect. Because of this, many campgrounds do not have water supplies. (Water availability is listed in the campground tables.) In the off-season, campground water supplies may be turned off to prevent freezing or because of a lack of funds to maintain them. If you plan to stay in a campground without a water supply, make sure you carry enough water in your vehicle to last your stay. During the hot half of the year (April through September), wise Arizona travelers carry at least a couple gallons of water in their vehicle in case of breakdown or becoming stranded. This is especially important for travel off paved highways. During hot weather in the desert, your survival time without water is measured in hours.

Late summer brings thunderstorms to the state. The accompanying lightning is dangerous, and you should take refuge in a safe place, such as your vehicle, during thunderstorms. If you're caught in the open, avoid lone trees and high ground. Find the lowest nearby area, and then squat on the ground with your feet together until the lightning passes. Heavy rain from thunderstorms can cause normally dry washes to suddenly flood, often miles from the storm, so never camp or park your vehicle in dry washes.

Winter weather is a hazard in the Arizona mountains from November through mid-April. A major winter storm can quickly cause highways to become snowpacked and icy, and make back roads completely impassable even to four-wheel-drive vehicles. Expect highway delays due to snow plowing and accidents. If you do travel and camp in the mountains during the winter season, be prepared with extra clothing, blankets or sleeping bags, extra food and water, and tire chains or a four-wheel-drive vehicle. Keep a close eye on the weather forecast. A small weather radio that picks up broadcasts directly from the National Weather Service is a good investment and often works in areas without cell phone coverage.

Mine Shafts

Arizona has always been attractive to miners and prospectors because of its vast expanses of bare, often-mineralized rock. As a result, abandoned mine shafts and prospect holes are common in many areas. While land managers and mining authorities are making an attempt to secure dangerous sites, the sheer size of the problem leaves a lot of hazards.

Never enter any mine shaft. Besides the obvious hazards of collapse, old mines often contain poisonous or radioactive gases as well as unstable explosives and dangerous equipment. Report any explosives or other unusual hazards to the land management agency after your trip. The presence of an old road, even if closed and now part of a designated wilderness, may be a sign that there are old mines in the area. Be especially alert for old mine shafts in heavy brush and at night. In areas that have attracted a lot of prospecting, miners often dug numerous small pits. Even though these pits are usually only a few feet deep, coming upon one unaware can result in ankle or leg injuries or worse. In mined areas, stay away from the edges of vertical shafts, even if covered. The edges of shafts often continue to crumble for years after abandonment. Also avoid depressions in the ground—these may mark shafts or pits that have been covered with wood or metal that is rotting or rusting away.

Animals and Other Creatures

Many Arizona campgrounds provide special opportunities for viewing wildlife. (These opportunities are mentioned in the campground descriptions.) Enjoy the wildlife, but please remember that you're a visitor in the outdoors when you're camping. What is a temporary outdoor home for you is the only home for wild animals and plants. Treat all wildlife with respect and caution. Most hazardous encounters with wild animals are a direct result of an irresponsible person.

Never approach or attempt to handle any wild animal. All animals will defend themselves if they feel threatened or cornered. Even rabbits will bite to protect their young. By approaching or harassing wildlife, you are placing great stress on the animal and endangering yourself. Never feed any wild animal, no matter how cute it seems. Human food is not good for them. Animals that become used to handouts lose their natural fear of humans and become camp robbers, endangering both you and your equipment.

Mountain Lions

Arizona mountain lions are rare and elusive creatures in the remote country where they still survive. You'll be lucky to see tracks, let alone the animal, and mountain lion encounters usually result in just a fleeting glimpse of this magnificent animal. The only cases of attack have been where the human aroused the lion's predatory instincts

Mountain lions are found mainly in remote, rugged mountains and canyons.

by appearing to be prey. Running and mountain biking in lion country seem to have a slight chance of evoking the same response that a running deer causes. If you do encounter a mountain lion, avoid prey-like reactions. Make yourself appear as big and threatening as possible, and make unnatural sounds by rattling metal pots or the like. Don't turn your back on the animal—and don't run.

Wolves and Coyotes

The native Mexican gray wolf has been reintroduced into the mountains of eastern Arizona. They are not a hazard to humans. Neither are coyotes. The thrilling nocturnal howl of coyotes is as much a part of the Arizona backcountry as are the clear, starry nights. We can only hope that the wolves are successful in their former ranges and that we will be lucky enough to hear their song as well.

Domestic Cattle

Public land, especially national forest, BLM, and state land, is often used for grazing, so you're likely to encounter cattle. Generally cattle are used to humans and will either avoid you or move away. It's possible that a bull could be dangerous, so it's a good idea to give cattle a reasonable margin. Grazing is generally not allowed in national parks and monuments.

Snakes and Other Reptiles

Arizona rattlesnakes are fascinating animals, well adapted for life in the harsh environment. Rattlesnakes do not attack people unless they feel threatened, although they may accidentally crawl in your direction if they're not aware of your presence. Rattlesnakes are more sensitive to ground vibrations than to sound, and they ordinarily move quietly away from an approaching large animal, such as a hiker. If surprised, they usually coil into a defensive posture and back slowly away. The snake creates its unmistakable buzzing rattle by shaking its tail so fast it blurs. When you hear the rattle, stop immediately and spot the snake before moving carefully away.

Never handle or tease any snake. Bites usually occur on the feet or hands, so never step or put your hands in places you can't see. Most rattlesnake bites are suffered by collectors. It's very rare for a camper to be bitten. Rattlesnake bites can be distinguished from nonpoisonous snake bites by the two puncture wounds left by the venom-injecting fangs, in addition to the regular tooth marks.

Never kill rattlesnakes. They're a vital part of the desert ecology and should be treated with respect, and not feared unnecessarily. Don't handle a dead rattlesnake; it can strike by reflex for some time after death.

The Sonoran coral snake is found only in the deserts of southern Arizona and northwestern Mexico. While extremely poisonous, it is reclusive and very small and would have difficulty biting a human.

All other snakes in Arizona are nonpoisonous, although they may bite if handled. Snakes prefer surfaces at about 80°F, so during hot weather they prefer the shade of bushes or rock overhangs and in cool weather will be found sunning themselves on open ground. During cold weather they are inactive. Any time lizards are active, rattlesnakes probably are active as well. Use a flashlight when moving around camp after dark, at least in the warmer months when snakes are active mainly at night. Never walk around camp barefoot or in sandals during that time of year.

A large lizard, the Gila monster, possesses venom similar to that of rattlesnakes, but it clamps on to its victim and grinds the venom into the wound with its molars. A rare and elusive reptile about a foot long that is protected by state law, the Gila monster is likely to bite only if handled or molested. Don't let its torpid appearance fool you—it can move very fast.

If someone in your party is bitten by a poisonous snake or a Gila monster, keep the victim calm and transport the person to a hospital as soon as possible.

Insects

Poisonous insects and spiders are actually a greater hazard in Arizona than rattlesnakes. The small, straw-colored desert scorpion likes to lurk under rocks and logs and can give a sting that is life threatening to children and the elderly. Black widow spiders, identifiable by the red hourglass-shaped mark on the underside, can inflict a dangerous bite. The brown spider (sometimes called the brown recluse) is pale tan or yellow and often has a violin-shaped mark on its head. It inflicts a bite that can cause extensive tissue damage at the site but is not generally life threatening. These bites seem minor at first but may become very painful after several hours. There is no specific field treatment; young children should be transported to a hospital as soon as possible.

The larger, more common scorpions have a painful sting but are not as dangerous as the small scorpions. The ferocious-looking centipede can produce a painful bite and can also irritate skin with its sharp, clawed feet, but it is not life threatening.

Scorpions, spiders, and centipedes can be almost completely avoided by taking a few simple precautions. Avoid placing your hands and feet where you cannot see them. Kick over rocks or logs before moving them with your hands. Don't unpack your sleeping bag before you need it in the evening, and always shake out clothing and footwear in the morning before dressing.

Kissing bugs, also known as cone-nose or assassin bugs, are obnoxious insects about ½ to 1 inch long and brown or black in color. They live in rodent nests and feed on mammal blood at night, leaving a large, itchy welt on the victim. They're only a problem if you sleep under the stars without a tent or other shelter.

Ticks occur rarely in Arizona. If ticks are discovered in your camping area, do a careful full-body search every day. It's important to remove embedded ticks before they have a chance to transmit disease, which takes a day or more.

Other insects such as bees, velvet ants, wasps, and the like give painful but non-threatening stings. The exception is for persons who have a known allergic reaction to specific insect stings. Such persons should carry insect sting kits prescribed by their doctors, since the reaction can develop rapidly and become life threatening.

Africanized honeybees were accidentally introduced into Brazil in the 1960s and have since spread north to Arizona. Encounters are most common in urban areas, but it's possible that a camper could encounter Africanized bees, especially in desert areas. Although the Africanized bee's venom is no more toxic than that of the common European honeybee, Africanized bees are more aggressive in defending their hives and will sometimes swarm on or chase an intruder.

Avoid all beehives. This includes cultivated bees, which may be a mixture of both types. Cultivated beehives are stacks of white boxes, always found near roads. Wild bees build hives in such places as rock crevices and holes in trees. Always avoid swarming bees. If attacked, protect your eyes and run away. If shelter such as a tent, vehicle, or building is available, use it; otherwise, head for heavy brush, which confuses bees. Africanized bees don't pursue more than 0.5 mile.

There are many scary-looking desert insects that, in reality, are not dangerous. Millipedes, whip scorpions, Jerusalem crickets, sun spiders, and tarantulas are examples of ferocious-looking creatures that are not a threat to humans.

Plants

Plant hazards are easily avoided. Never eat any plant, unless you are an expert and know what you're doing. Some areas have stinging nettles, which as the name implies, don't feel good on the skin. Check carefully before sitting or lying on the ground in nettle areas. Poison ivy grows seasonally along streams and moist drainages at about 4,000 to 6,000 feet in Arizona. The organic acid on the leaves and stems causes a severe skin reaction in many people and passes easily from one object to another. If exposed, wash all clothing, equipment, pets, and your skin thoroughly. Poison ivy is easily recognized by its shiny green leaves which grow in groups of three.

Slow-growing desert plants have developed an interesting array of defenses to protect themselves and their precious moisture from animals, birds, and insects that would like to dine on them. Spines and thorns are some of the obvious features of cactus and cactus-like plants. Most spines are needle-like and cause simple punctures. Teddy bear cholla, also known as jumping cholla, which is found in the Sonoran Desert of central and southwestern Arizona, looks cute and cuddly but it's not. Each branch is covered with thousands of slender spines, each of which has invisible barbs. If a burr sticks to your skin or clothing, remove it with a pocket comb or a pair of sticks. Then use a good pair of tweezers to pick out the remaining spines. If the spines become deeply embedded, the victim should seek medical attention.

Use care around plants with large, spine-tipped leaves, such as agaves and yuccas. The spines can cause deep puncture wounds if you accidentally stumble into them or grab one as a handhold. The edges of the stiff leaves often have hooked thorns that can cause nasty scratches or deeper wounds. Some small cacti, such as the aptly named pincushion cactus, are small and straw colored and tend to hide in grass. They are a particular hazard when you're scrambling up rocky areas.

Catclaw is a bush that sometimes grows in dense thickets. The sharp, curved thorns catch on clothing and skin and have to be carefully peeled off. Long-sleeved shirts and pants help, but it's best to avoid the thickets altogether.

Emergency Phone Numbers

The statewide emergency services number is 911. Use 911 only in an emergency. If you have a nonemergency call, use the administrative phone number for the agency you want. Some general numbers are listed in the text; the phone number of the managing agency of each campground is listed in the information block for that campground.

For the Arizona Highway Patrol, county sheriff's departments, and the National Weather Service, refer to your local phone book for the phone numbers in each area. For statewide road conditions, call 511 or go to www.az511.com.

Camping Etiquette

Picking a Campsite

Try to arrive at your chosen campground early so that you'll have plenty of time to find a good site. When you enter the campground, check the bulletin board or entrance station for instructions and any special regulations and to pay the campground fee. Many campgrounds are self-serve. In this case, drive around the campground until you find a site you like. Leave someone, or a piece of gear such as a cooler, at the campsite so that others will know that it's occupied while you go back to the entrance and pay the fee.

If you arrive late at the campground, avoid excessive driving around while looking for a site—and dim your headlights. Your fellow campers will appreciate it.

Zero Impact

Always use trash receptacles. If the campground does not have trash removal services, you must carry out all your trash. Never bury food scraps, packaging, or any sort of trash. Animals will dig up anything with a food odor. Never burn trash in a campfire. Many packaging materials contain thin layers of aluminum, which does not burn in even the hottest campfire. Like plastic, it fuses into small blobs. Popular camping areas are scarred with numerous old fire pits that glitter with bits of aluminum and plastic. Also, most plastics give off highly toxic fumes when burned.

Carry out trash left by careless or thoughtless people, especially when camping away from developed campgrounds. A few extra garbage bags and a pair of gloves will come in handy for this task—and then you can bask in the glow of self-righteous pleasure!

Campfire Restrictions

Campfire restrictions may be in effect during periods of high fire danger. Although fire restrictions usually apply only to campfires outside developed campgrounds, in some cases campfires may be prohibited in designated campsites as well. Even if restrictions are not in place, never build a fire on a windy day or at any other time you perceive the fire danger to be high.

Extinguishing Your Campfire

State and federal law requires you to completely extinguish your campfire before leaving it unattended. Two campers failed to do so during the summer of 2011, and the result was the second-largest wildfire in American history, the Wallow Fire which burned over half a million acres of beautiful forest in eastern Arizona.

To put out your campfire, mix the coals and ashes with water until it is cold to the touch. The most effective technique is to add a little water at a time and stir·the ashes well before adding more water. You must be able to put your bare hand in the ashes—to do this safely, start by feeling the fire with the back of your hand held a few inches above the ashes. If you don't feel heat, then you can feel the ashes with your fingers.

If you're dispersed camping and water is short, you can use dirt, but it will take much longer to cool down your fire. Never put a fire out with dirt in a campground or in a fire pit that others will reuse.

It can't be emphasized too strongly that just pouring water over a fire or covering it with dirt *does not put it out*. The fire continues to burn under the top layer of wet ashes or under a layer of dirt and can easily escape later.

Stay Limits and Checkout Time

Nearly all campgrounds have posted stay limits, usually from seven to fourteen days. A few very popular sites have shorter stay limits, while designated long-term camping areas may allow stays of several months. Many campgrounds impose limits on the number of persons that may occupy a campsite. The number of vehicles may be limited as well. Please observe the stay limit so that other campers can have their turn. Always observe the posted checkout time. If you have to stay later, check with the campground host or ranger to see if you need to pay an additional night's fee.

Picnicking in Campgrounds

Never use campsites for picnicking. Some campgrounds have designated day-use areas; otherwise, use a picnic area for day use.

Respect Other Persons

At all times, respect other persons and treat them as you would like to be treated. During the busy season, some campgrounds can become crowded. Respect other campers' desire for privacy. Think about your neighbors before you light that lantern or shine that flashlight around. Most campgrounds have posted quiet hours, which are usually between 10 p.m. and 6 a.m. During quiet hours avoid disturbing other campers; do not run generators, play radios or stereos, or make other loud noises.

Share Space

All campgrounds have shared facilities, which may include restrooms, water taps, trash bins, sanitary disposal stations, and other facilities. Patiently wait your turn when other campers are ahead of you. Remember, part of the idea of camping is to leave the frantic pace of the city behind and exchange it for a more relaxed lifestyle!

Map Legend

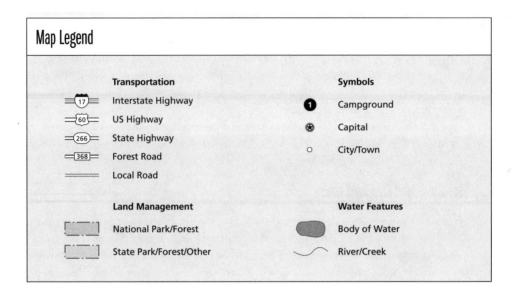

Transportation

≡(17)≡   Interstate Highway

≡(60)≡   US Highway

≡(266)≡   State Highway

≡[368]≡   Forest Road

═══   Local Road

Land Management

National Park/Forest

State Park/Forest/Other

Symbols

❶   Campground

✷   Capital

○   City/Town

Water Features

Body of Water

River/Creek

Canyon Country

Arizona's Canyon Country includes the southwestern section of the Colorado Plateau, a vast land of deep canyons and high plateaus. It includes the North and South Rims of the Grand Canyon, the volcanic mountain country around Flagstaff and Williams, and the canyon-carved edge of the western Mogollon Rim. The Grand Canyon's mile-deep, 300-mile-long barrier isolates the plateau to the north from the rest of Arizona. On the east, at the upper end of the canyons, US 89A crosses the Colorado River near the historic site of Lees Ferry. The next crossing of the river and the canyons is 300 miles downstream at Hoover Dam on US 93.

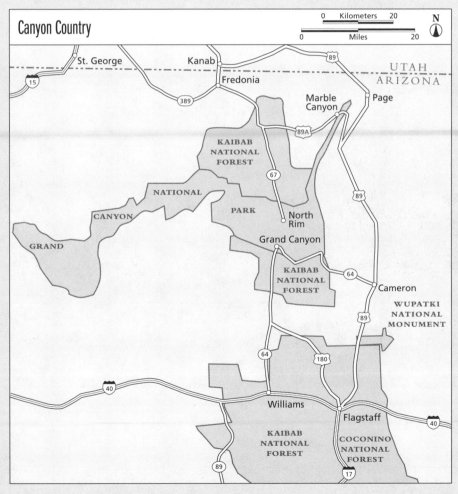

North Rim

The North Rim country is also known as the Arizona Strip because of its isolation from the rest of Arizona. It often seems more a part of Utah than Arizona. The BLM's Virgin River Campground is located on I-15 where it slices through the very northwest corner of Arizona on its way from Nevada to Utah. Get just a mile or so away from the busy freeway, and you're in the Arizona of fifty or one hundred years ago. Because of its distance from major population centers, the North Rim country is an uncrowded land. If you're looking to get away from crowds, this is the place. Even the Grand Canyon's North Rim is less busy than the South Rim. A star attraction for the camper is the high Kaibab Plateau, covered with an alpine forest of ponderosa pine, Douglas fir, and quaking aspen. *Kaibab* is an old Paiute Indian word meaning "mountain lying down," and that's a perfect description of this vast plateau.

For more information:
Fredonia Chamber of Commerce
www.fredoniaaz.net/Tourism/ChamberofCommerce.aspx

Angels Window Overlook on the Cape Royal Road

North Rim

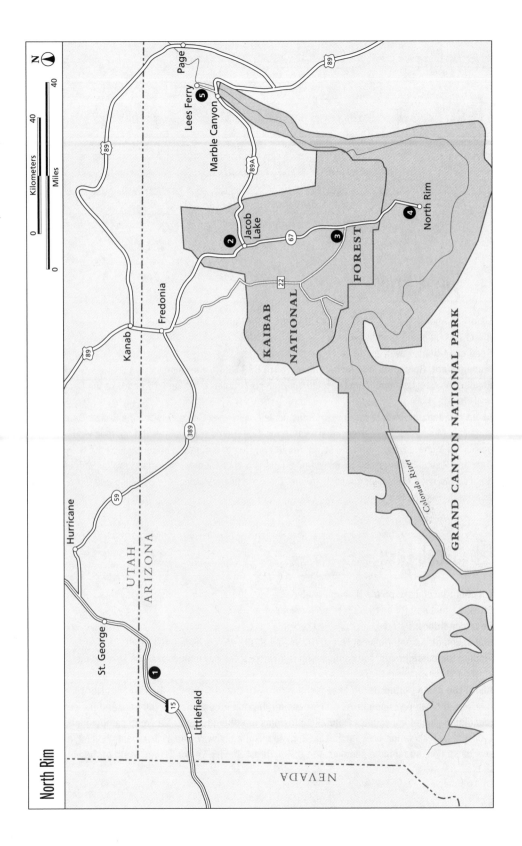

NEVADA

UTAH
ARIZONA

St. George

Hurricane

Littlefield

Kanab

Fredonia

Jacob Lake

Marble Canyon

Lees Ferry

Page

North Rim

KAIBAB NATIONAL FOREST

GRAND CANYON NATIONAL PARK

Colorado River

N

0   40   Kilometers
0   40   Miles

Number	Name	Elevation	Season	RV/Trailer	Sites	Water	RV dump	Fishing	Hiking trails	Boating	Boat launch	Wheelchair access	Fee	Stay limit, days
1	Virgin River	1,900	Year-round	•	75	•			•				•	14
2	Jacob Lake	7,900	May–Oct	•	51	•			•			•	•	14
3	DeMotte Park	9,000	May–Oct	•	38	•							•	14
4	North Rim	8,200	May–Oct	•	83	•			•				•	7
5	Lees Ferry	3,170	Year-round	•	54	•	•	•	•	•	•		•	14

1 Virgin River

Location: About 16 miles northeast of Littlefield, in the Virgin River Canyon

Sites: 75 tent and RV; no hookups

Road conditions: Paved

Management: Bureau of Land Management, (435) 688-3200, www.blm.gov

Finding the campground: From Littlefield, Arizona, go 16 miles north on I-15 and take the Cedar Pockets exit.

About the campground: Located in the spectacular Virgin River Gorge between the Beaver Dam and Virgin Mountains, this campground's canyon setting seems especially wild if approached across the Mohave Desert from the south. The freeway forms a narrow corridor through the Beaver Dam and Paiute Wildernesses, so this campground is a good base for hiking and exploring. There are also two short trails near the campground. There are limited services in Littlefield and full services in St. George, Utah.

2 Jacob Lake

Location: Jacob Lake on the Kaibab Plateau

Sites: 51 tent and RV up to 32 feet; no hookups

Road conditions: Paved

Management: Kaibab National Forest, (928) 635-8200, www.fs.usda.gov/kaibab

Finding the campground: The campground is located at the tiny hamlet of Jacob Lake, at the junction of US 89A and AZ 67.

About the campground: Jacob Lake is the gateway to Grand Canyon National Park's North Rim, and the campground makes a fine base for daylong excursions into the park and the surrounding high plateau country. Naturalist programs are offered. There is a group campground, available by reservation only. Jacob Lake Inn, across the highway, has a restaurant, lodging, a service station, and limited supplies. The USDA Forest Service Visitor Center, south of the inn,

Red rock formations along the Virgin River

can supply maps and information on the Kaibab National Forest. The nearest full services are in Fredonia and Kanab.

3 DeMotte Park

Location: About 25 miles south of Jacob Lake, on the Kaibab Plateau
Sites: 38 tent and RV up to 22 feet; no hookups
Road conditions: Paved, dirt
Management: Kaibab National Forest, (928) 635-8200, www.fs.usda.gov/kaibab
Finding the campground: From Jacob Lake on US 89A, go 25 miles south on AZ 67. Turn right just after passing Kaibab Lodge.
About the campground: The campground is set in the forest on the edge of DeMotte Park, the largest of several beautiful alpine meadows on the Kaibab Plateau. The campground makes a perfect base for exploring the plateau as well as Grand Canyon National Park just to the south. Naturalist programs are available. Kaibab Lodge has lodging and a restaurant, and North Rim Country Store across the highway has limited supplies and a service station. The nearest full services are in Fredonia and Kanab.

Bright Angel Point near North Rim Campground, Grand Canyon

4 North Rim

Location: North Rim of the Grand Canyon
Sites: 83 tent and RV; no hookups
Road conditions: Paved
Management: Grand Canyon National Park, (928) 638-7888, www.nps.gov/grca; reservations (877) 444-6777, www.recreation.gov
Finding the campground: From Jacob Lake on US 89A, go 43 miles south on AZ 67 to North Rim Village in Grand Canyon National Park.
About the campground: Although frequently full during summer, this campground's location is hard to beat as a base for enjoying and exploring the Grand Canyon's North Rim. It is the only campground at the North Rim. Lodging, restaurants, limited supplies, a dump station, and a service station are nearby. The nearest full services are in Fredonia and Kanab.

5 Lees Ferry

Location: Marble Canyon
Sites: 54 tent and RV; no hookups
Road conditions: Paved
Management: Glen Canyon National Recreation Area, (928) 608-6200, www.nps.gov/glca
Finding the campground: From Page, drive 25 miles south on US 89, and then turn right onto US 89A. Go 14 miles north to Marble Canyon; turn right onto Lees Ferry Road and continue 5 miles to the campground.
About the campground: Historic Lees Ferry was a major crossing point on the Colorado River until the ferry was replaced by Navajo Bridge in the 1920s. Hoover Dam, 300 miles downstream, is the next vehicle crossing on the Colorado River. Today Lees Ferry is famous for its trout fishery, created by the cold water issuing from the depths of Lake Powell, behind Glen Canyon Dam. Lees Ferry is also the launch point for Grand Canyon raft trips. The setting is dramatic, under the towering sandstone Vermilion and Echo Cliffs. Limited services, including gas, groceries, lodging, a restaurant, fishing guides, and a Laundromat, are available at Marble Canyon; the nearest full services are in Page.

South Rim

The Grand Canyon's South Rim is by far the more accessible and popular of the two rims, and campground spaces are hard to come by during summer. A good alternative is to stay in one of the campgrounds near Williams or Flagstaff and plan on a day trip to the South Rim. Off-season, the South Rim is less crowded, and it's possible to stay in Mather Campground, leave your vehicle parked, and explore the canyon's rim by shuttle bus and foot.

For more information:
Grand Canyon Chamber of Commerce
PO Box 3007
Grand Canyon, AZ 86023
(888) 472-2696
www.grandcanyoncvb.org

Sunset near Mather Campground, Grand Canyon

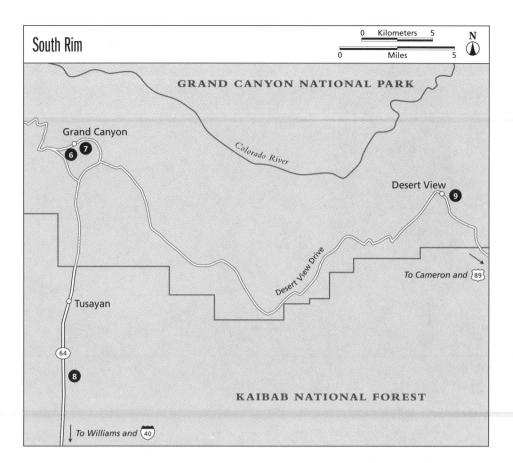

South Rim

Number	Name	Elevation	Season	RV/Trailer	Sites	Water	RV dump	Fishing	Hiking trails	Boating	Boat launch	Wheelchair access	Fee	Stay limit, days
6	Mather	7,100	Year-round	•	300+	•	•		•			•	•	7
7	Trailer Village	7,100	Year-round	•	78	•	•		•			•	•	
8	Ten-X	6,600	May–Sept	•	70	•			•			•	•	14
9	Desert View	7,400	May–Oct	•	50	•						•	•	7

Desert View Watchtower on the South Rim of the Grand Canyon

6 Mather

Location: Grand Canyon Village
Sites: 300+ tent and RV; no hookups
Road conditions: Paved
Management: Grand Canyon National Park, (928) 638-7888, www.nps.gov/grca; reservations (877) 444-6777, www.recreation.gov
Finding the campground: Mather campground is located across from the visitor center in Grand Canyon Village.
About the campground: The park's main campground, it is centrally located in Grand Canyon Village. Shuttle service is available in the village year-round, and along the Hermit Road except during the winter. There are hiking trails along the canyon rim and into the gorge. In season, the campground fills early. Lodging, restaurants, and a supermarket are nearby. Ground and air tours are available. The nearest full services are in Williams and Flagstaff.

7 Trailer Village

Location: Grand Canyon Village
Sites: 78 RV with full hookups
Road conditions: Paved
Management: Grand Canyon National Park, (928) 638-7888, www.nps.gov/grca; reservations (877) 444-6777, www.recreation.gov
Finding the campground: Trailer Village is located across from the visitor center in Grand Canyon Village.
About the campground: Trailer Village is centrally located in Grand Canyon Village, which has lodging, restaurants, and a supermarket. The nearest full services are in Williams and Flagstaff.

8 Ten-X

Location: Grand Canyon's South Rim
Sites: 70 tent and RV up to 22 feet; no hookups
Road conditions: Paved
Management: Kaibab National Forest, (928) 635-8200, www.fs.usda.gov/kaibab; reservations (877) 444-6777, www.recreation.gov
Finding the campground: From Williams, drive north 49 miles on AZ 64; turn right at the campground sign. The campground is 2.5 miles south of Tusayan.
About the campground: This USDA Forest Service campground is a good alternative to camping in Grand Canyon National Park, which is 4 miles north. During September it's a good place to sleep after Grand Canyon Music Festival concerts on the South Rim. You also have a good chance of seeing and hearing elk near this campground. The campground features a nature

trail, and group campsites are available. Lodging, restaurants, service stations, and supplies are available in Tusayan and Grand Canyon Village. The nearest full services are in Williams and Flagstaff.

9 Desert View

Location: Grand Canyon's South Rim
Sites: 50 tent and RV; no hookups
Road conditions: Paved
Management: Grand Canyon National Park, (928) 638-7888, www.nps.gov/grca; reservations (877) 444-6777, www.recreation.gov

Finding the campground: From Grand Canyon Village, drive 25 miles east on East Rim Drive to Desert View. From Cameron on US 89, drive west 32 miles on AZ 64. The campground is 0.25 mile north of the East Entrance Station.

About the campground: Desert View is famous for its unique view of the Grand Canyon, the Colorado River, and the Painted Desert to the east. Several other viewpoints offer fine views of the canyon. The small village has minimal services—a snack bar, a service station, and limited supplies. The nearest full services are in Flagstaff.

Point Moran along Desert View Drive, Grand Canyon

Williams

The town of Williams, "Gateway to the Grand Canyon," was named for mountain man Bill Williams, a famous master trapper and scout on the Santa Fe Trail. Its western heritage is still evident along its historic district, where the Grand Canyon Railway even offers an opportunity to ride a steam-engine train to the Grand Canyon. Located on the high, cool Coconino Plateau, Williams and the surrounding area are popular summer recreation destinations. Several reservoirs supply water for the town, and boating and fishing opportunities for recreationists. Three hiking trails lead to the summit of Bill Williams Mountain, just south of town, and the backcountry of Sycamore Canyon Wilderness lies southeast of town, near White Horse Lake.

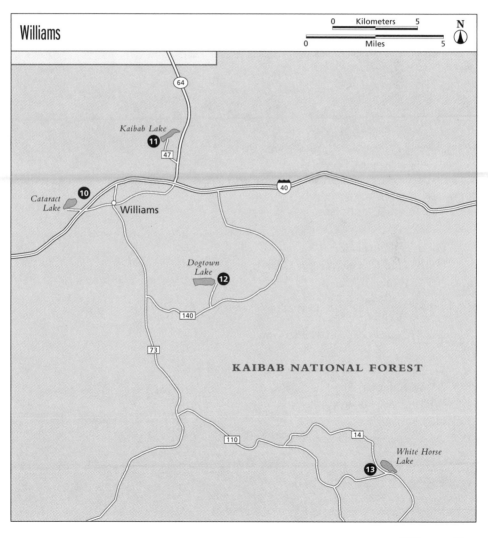

Dogtown Lake

For more information:
USDA Forest Service Visitor Center
200 W. Railhead Ave.
Williams, AZ 86046
(928) 635-8200
www.fs.usda.gov/main/kaibab/home

Williams–Grand Canyon Chamber of Commerce
200 W. Railroad Ave.
Williams, AZ 86046
(928) 635-1418
www.experiencewilliams.com

Number	Name	Elevation	Season	RV/Trailer	Sites	Water	RV dump	Fishing	Hiking trails	Boating	Boat launch	Wheelchair access	Fee	Stay limit, days
10	Cataract Lake	6,800	May–Sept	•	18	•		•	•	•	•	•	•	14
11	Kaibab Lake	6,800	May–Sept	•	73	•		•	•	•	•	•	•	14
12	Dogtown Lake	7,000	May–Sept	•	51	•		•	•	•	•	•	•	14
13	White Horse Lake	6,600	May–Sept	•	85	•		•	•	•	•	•	•	14

10 Cataract Lake

Location: Williams
Sites: 18 tent and RV up to 18 feet; no hookups
Road conditions: Paved
Management: Kaibab National Forest, (928) 635-8200, www.fs.usda.gov/kaibab
Finding the campground: From Williams, drive west on Bill Williams Avenue, passing under I-40.
About the campground: This small campground is convenient to Williams, where full services are available. Boating (limited to 1 hp electric motors) and fishing are popular on the lake. Nearby Bill Williams Mountain has several hiking trails, and miles of forest roads provide opportunities for mountain biking and exploring.

11 Kaibab Lake

Location: Williams
Sites: 73 tent and RV up to 22 feet; no hookups
Road conditions: Paved
Management: Kaibab National Forest, (928) 635-8200, www.fs.usda.gov/kaibab; reservations (877) 444-6777, www.recreation.gov
Finding the campground: From Williams, go 1 mile east on I-40, and exit north on AZ 64. Continue 1 more mile; turn left onto FR 47, and go 1 mile to the campground.
About the campground: Boating (limited to 1 hp electric motors) and fishing are available on Kaibab Lake. The campground makes a good base for day trips to Grand Canyon National Park and for exploring the forested Coconino Plateau and the mountains south of Williams. There are evening interpretive programs in season. Full services are available in nearby Williams.

An old logging railroad bed near Dogtown Lake

12 Dogtown Lake

Location: About 7 miles southeast of Williams, on the Coconino Plateau

Sites: 51 tent and RV up to 22 feet; no hookups

Road conditions: Paved, all-weather dirt

Management: Kaibab National Forest, (928) 635-8200, www.fs.usda.gov/kaibab; reservations (877) 444-6777, www.recreation.gov

Finding the campground: From Williams, drive 4 miles south on Perkinsville Road, CR 73, and then turn left onto FR 140. Go 2.5 miles; turn left on FR 132 and continue less than a mile to the campground.

About the campground: Dogtown Lake is popular with boaters and anglers. The campground has a short nature trail, and a longer hiking trail takes you to the top of Davenport Hill. There are many other hiking trails on nearby Bill Williams Mountain and in Sycamore Canyon Wilderness to the south. The forest road system provides plenty of opportunities for exploring and mountain biking. Full services are available in Williams.

13 White Horse Lake

Location: About 17 miles southeast of Williams, near Sycamore Canyon

Sites: 85 tent and RV up to 22 feet; no hookups

Road conditions: Paved, all-weather dirt

Management: Kaibab National Forest, (928) 635-8200, www.fs.usda.gov/kaibab; reservations (877) 444-6777, www.recreation.gov

Finding the campground: From Williams, drive 8 miles south on Perkinsville Road, CR 73, and then turn left onto FR 110. Go 7 miles; turn left on FR 109 and go 2 miles to the lake and campground.

About the campground: White Horse Lake features boating (limited to 1 hp electric motors) and is very popular with anglers. The campground is an ideal base for exploring the western Mogollon Rim country and the forested plateau. FR 110 continues south of the campground to Sycamore Point, a dramatic viewpoint overlooking the rugged Sycamore Canyon Wilderness. Miles of other forest roads are great for mountain biking. Full services are available in Williams.

Flagstaff

The largest city in northern Arizona, Flagstaff has a full range of visitor services, as well as cultural events and museums. Spend some time at the Museum of Northern Arizona to learn more about the natural and human history of the area. The Arboretum at Flagstaff has nine gardens that display plants native to the area, including thirty rare and endangered species. Lowell Observatory, where the dwarf planet Pluto was first discovered, also has an excellent visitor center.

The Coconino Plateau surrounding Flagstaff is heavily forested with ponderosa pine. The high mountain elevation provides a welcome respite from the heat of the deserts below. The highest mountain in the state, 12,633-foot San Francisco Mountain, known locally as the San Francisco Peaks, dominates the skyline to the north. The majestic summits are the home of the gods in both the Navajo and Hopi religions and are the largest of more than 600 volcanoes in the area. Nearby Sunset

The San Francisco Peaks above Lockett Meadow Campground

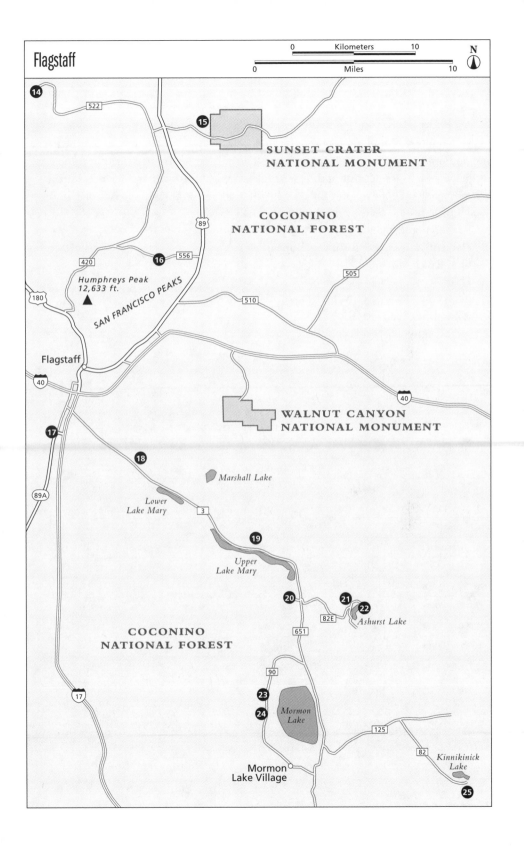

Flagstaff

0 Kilometers 10
0 Miles 10

N

14

522

15

SUNSET CRATER
NATIONAL MONUMENT

COCONINO
NATIONAL FOREST

89

420 **16** 556

505

*Humphreys Peak
12,633 ft.*

SAN FRANCISCO PEAKS

510

180

Flagstaff

40

40

WALNUT CANYON
NATIONAL MONUMENT

17

18

89A

Marshall Lake

*Lower
Lake Mary*

3

19

*Upper
Lake Mary*

20 **21** **22**

82E *Ashurst Lake*

651

COCONINO
NATIONAL FOREST

90

23

24 *Mormon
Lake*

125

17

82 *Kinnikinick
Lake*

Mormon
Lake Village

25

Crater National Monument preserves the results of the most recent volcanic eruption. Walnut Canyon and Wupatki National Monuments provide a chance for visitors to view some of the ancient dwellings used by the Sinagua Indians and understand how they lived.

Southeast of the city lies a section of the Mogollon Plateau known locally as "Lake Country." Numerous lakes on this high, forested plateau support angling, boating, and other water sports. The plateau ends abruptly at the south-facing escarpment of the Mogollon Rim. Most of the forest is laced with dirt roads, and it's a mountain biker's paradise. There are also miles of hiking trails, most notably the Arizona Trail, which traverses the region on its way from Utah to Mexico.

For more information:
Flagstaff Convention & Visitors Bureau
One East Route 66
Flagstaff, AZ 86001
(928) 774-9541; (800) 842-7293
www.flagstaffarizona.org
visitorcenter@flagstaffaz.gov

Number	Name	Elevation	Season	RV/Trailer	Sites	Water	RV dump	Fishing	Hiking trails	Boating	Boat launch	Wheelchair access	Fee	Stay limit, days
14	Lockett Meadow	8,600	July–Sept		17				•				•	14
15	Bonito	6,900	May–Oct	•	44	•			•			•	•	14
16	Little Elden Spring Horse Camp	7,200	May–Oct	•	15	•			•				•	14
17	Fort Tuthill County Park	6,900	May–Sept	•	75	•			•			•	•	14
18	Canyon Vista	6,900	May–Oct	•	11	•			•				•	14
19	Lakeview	6,900	May–Sept	•	30	•		•	•	•		•	•	14
20	Pinegrove	6,900	May–Sept	•	46	•		•	•			•	•	14
21	Ashurst Lake	7,000	May–Sept	•	25	•		•	•	•	•	•	•	14
22	Forked Pine	7,100	May–Sept	•	25	•		•	•	•	•	•	•	14
23	Dairy Springs	7,000	May–Sept	•	30	•		•	•			•	•	14
24	Double Springs	7,000	May–Sept	•	15	•		•	•			•	•	14
25	Kinnikinick Lake	7,000	May–Sept	•	13	•		•	•	•	•		•	14

Aspen trees soften the landscape near Lockett Meadow Campground, San Francisco Peaks.

14 Lockett Meadow

Location: About 17 miles north of Flagstaff

Sites: 17 tent

Road conditions: Dirt

Management: Coconino National Forest, (928) 527-3620, www.fs.usda.gov/main/coconino/home

Finding the campground: From Flagstaff, drive about 12 miles north on US 89, and turn left onto FR 420. This turnoff is opposite the Sunset Crater National Monument turnoff. Go 0.5 mile, and turn right on FR 522. Continue 4.2 miles to the end of the road at the campground.

About the campground: The campground is located in an aspen grove at the edge of Lockett Meadow at the foot of the San Francisco Peaks' scenic Interior Valley, a glacial canyon carved through the heart of the mountain. The Inner Basin Trail leads up the valley and connects to a network of trails, some of which are open to mountain bikers. It is a great base for day hikes and rides on the mountain.

Sunflowers in Bonito Park, Sunset Crater National Monument

15 Bonito

Location: About 16 miles north of Flagstaff, at Sunset Crater National Monument
Sites: 44 tent and RV up to 22 feet; no hookups
Road conditions: Paved
Management: Coconino National Forest, (928) 527-3620, www.fs.usda.gov/main/coconino/home
Finding the campground: From Flagstaff, drive about 14 miles north on US 89, and turn right onto the Sunset Crater road, FR 545. Go 2 miles and turn left into the campground.
About the campground: Located next to Sunset Crater National Monument, Bonito Campground is named for the nearby Bonito Lava Flow, which erupted from the base of Sunset Crater Volcano less than 1,000 years ago. The campground is in an open stand of ponderosa pines in a lunar-like landscape—a great place to watch the full moon rise. The nearby Park Service visitor center explains the volcanic history of the area. Naturalist programs are available. Several trails provide access to viewpoints and natural features. Nearby Wupatki National Monument features ruins from a Native American culture that thrived in the area northeast of Sunset Crater. The nearest full services are in Flagstaff.

16 Little Elden Spring Horse Camp

Location: About 7 miles north of Flagstaff, at the base of Mount Elden
Sites: 15 tent and RV up to 35 feet; no hookups
Road conditions: Dirt
Management: Coconino National Forest, (928) 527-3620, www.fs.usda.gov/main/coconino/home; reservations (877) 444-6777, www.recreation.gov
Finding the campground: From Flagstaff, drive about 5 miles north on US 89. Turn left onto FR 556 and continue 2 miles to the campground.
About the campground: This campground is open to equestrians only. It's ideally placed at a trailhead for the extensive Mount Elden–Dry Lake Hills trail system, which is popular with mountain bikers and hikers as well as equestrians. The campground is in a pleasant stand of ponderosa pine and Gambel oak below the 2,000-foot east slopes of Mount Elden. The nearest full services are in Flagstaff.

17 Fort Tuthill County Park

Location: Flagstaff
Sites: 75 tent and RV up to 35 feet; a few hookups
Road conditions: Paved
Management: Coconino County Parks and Recreation, (928) 679-8000, www.coconino.az.gov/parks.aspx?id=410
Finding the campground: From Flagstaff, drive 2 miles south on I-17, and exit at AZ 89A. Turn right (west) into the park and campground.
About the campground: Site of the annual Coconino County Fair and numerous other events, the park features the campground, picnic areas, and a country store. The campground makes a fine base for exploring in and around Flagstaff, as well as Oak Creek Canyon 12 miles to the south on AZ 89A. Full services are available in nearby Flagstaff.

18 Canyon Vista

Location: About 6 miles southeast of Flagstaff, on Lake Mary Road
Sites: 11 tent and RV up to 22 feet; no hookups
Road conditions: Paved
Management: Coconino National Forest, (928) 527-3620, www.fs.usda.gov/main/coconino/home
Finding the campground: From Flagstaff, drive 6 miles southeast on Lake Mary Road, CR 3; turn left into the campground.
About the campground: Hiking trails and rock climbing are this scenic pine-forested campground's main attractions. The two boat ramps on Upper Lake Mary are just to the south, and the lake is popular with anglers and water-skiers during the summer. Full services are available in Flagstaff, and there are limited supplies at the north end of Lower Lake Mary.

19 Lakeview

Location: About 11 miles southeast of Flagstaff, on Upper Lake Mary
Sites: 30 tent and RV up to 26 feet; no hookups
Road conditions: Paved
Management: Coconino National Forest, (928) 527-3620, www.fs.usda.gov/main/coconino/home
Finding the campground: From Flagstaff, drive 11 miles southeast on Lake Mary Road, CR 3; turn left into the campground.
About the campground: Fishing and boating on Upper Lake Mary are two of this scenic pine-forested campground's attractions. Full services are available in Flagstaff, and there are limited supplies at the north end of Lower Lake Mary. Both lakes are good sites for wildlife viewing, including migrating waterfowl, bald eagles, and resident ospreys. Elk are common in the area.

20 Pinegrove

Location: About 16 miles southeast of Flagstaff, near Upper Lake Mary
Sites: 46 tent and RV up to 45 feet; no hookups
Road conditions: Paved
Management: Coconino National Forest, (928) 527-3620, www.fs.usda.gov/main/coconino/home; reservations (877) 444-6777, www.recreation.gov
Finding the campground: From Flagstaff, drive 16 miles southeast on Lake Mary Road, CR 3. Turn right onto FR 651, and continue 0.5 mile to the campground.
About the campground: Located in northern Arizona's pine-forested lake country, the campground can serve as a base for trips to most of the lakes in the area. Left over from the last ice age, many of the natural lakes on this high plateau have been augmented with small dams and are popular with boaters and anglers. Limited services are available at Mormon Lake Village, 10 miles south; full services are available in Flagstaff.

21 Ashurst Lake

Location: About 21 miles southeast of Flagstaff, on Ashurst Lake
Sites: 25 tent and RV up to 35 feet; no hookups
Road conditions: Paved
Management: Coconino National Forest, (928) 527-3620, www.fs.usda.gov/main/coconino/home
Finding the campground: From Flagstaff, drive 16 miles southeast on Lake Mary Road, CR 3. Turn left (east) onto Ashurst Lake Road, FR 82E, and continue 5 miles to the campground.
About the campground: Ashurst Lake is popular with boaters and anglers. Because the lake tends to be breezy, it's also a destination for sailboarders. It's also a great place to view wildlife, including waterfowl, hawks, and songbirds. The duck watching is especially good—it's a real quack fest. The campground is on Anderson Mesa, in an open forest of ponderosa pine, piñon pine, and juniper. Limited services are available at Mormon Lake Village, 15 miles south; full services are available in Flagstaff.

22 Forked Pine

Location: About 22 miles southeast of Flagstaff, on Ashurst Lake
Sites: 25 tent and RV up to 35 feet; no hookups
Road conditions: Paved
Management: Coconino National Forest, (928) 527-3620, www.fs.usda.gov/main/coconino/home
Finding the campground: From Flagstaff, drive 16 miles southeast on Lake Mary Road, CR 3. Turn left onto Ashurst Lake Road, FR 82E, and continue 6 miles to the campground.
About the campground: This is the second campground at Ashurst Lake, located on the northeast shore.

There are many hiking trails on the San Francisco Peaks near Flagstaff.

23 Dairy Springs

Location: About 24 miles southeast of Flagstaff, on Mormon Lake

Sites: 30 tent and RV up to 35 feet; no hookups

Road conditions: Paved

Management: Coconino National Forest, (928) 527-3620, www.fs.usda.gov/main/coconino/home; reservations (877) 444-6777, www.recreation.gov

Finding the campground: From Flagstaff, drive 20 miles southeast on Lake Mary Road, CR 3, and turn right onto Mormon Lake Road, FR 90. Continue 4 miles to the campground, which is on the right.

About the campground: The campground is located in a stand of ponderosa pines across the road from Mormon Lake, the largest natural lake in Arizona. Most of the year the lake is actually a shallow marsh, but that makes it a prime spot for wildlife viewing. Several trails start from the campground and lead to scenic overlooks. Group camping is available. Mormon Lake has limited fishing. Some supplies and a restaurant are available in Mormon Lake Village, 4 miles south. Full services are available in Flagstaff.

24 Double Springs

Location: About 25 miles southeast of Flagstaff, on Mormon Lake
Sites: 15 tent and RV up to 35 feet; no hookups
Road conditions: Paved
Management: Coconino National Forest, (928) 527-3620, www.fs.usda.gov/main/coconino/home
Finding the campground: From Flagstaff, drive 20 miles southeast on Lake Mary Road, CR 3, and turn right onto Mormon Lake Road, FR 90. Continue 5 miles to the campground, which is on the right.
About the campground: This campground is just down the road from Dairy Springs Campground and is also across the road from Mormon Lake, in tall pines. Mormon Lake has limited fishing. A short hiking trail leads to a rock ledge with a good view of Mormon Lake. Some supplies and a restaurant are available in Mormon Lake Village, 3 miles south. Full services are available in Flagstaff.

25 Kinnikinick Lake

Location: About 35 miles southeast of Flagstaff, at Kinnikinick Lake
Sites: 13 tent and RV up to 22 feet; no hookups
Road conditions: Dirt
Management: Coconino National Forest, (928) 527-3620, www.fs.usda.gov/main/coconino/home
Finding the campground: From Flagstaff, drive 25 miles southeast on Lake Mary Road, CR 3, and turn left onto FR 125. Go 5 miles and turn right onto FR 82, the main road. Continue another 5 miles to the campground, which is on the left.
About the campground: The campground is on the shore of Kinnikinick Lake, on a high grassy plateau with scattered ponderosa pine, piñon pine, and juniper. As with the other lakeside campgrounds, this is a good spot for wildlife viewing, including bald eagles, elk, and antelope. Limited services are available at Mormon Lake Village; the nearest full services are in Flagstaff.

Indian Country

I ndian Country is a vast and colorful land, a part of the Colorado Plateau bordered on the north by Lake Powell and the San Juan River, on the west by the Grand Canyon, New Mexico on the east, and I-40 on the south. It is the home of the Navajo Nation, the largest Native American reservation in the United States, covering one-sixth of Arizona and extending into three neighboring states. Many Navajo still live as herders of sheep, goats, cattle, and horses. Although most Navajo families live in modern houses, some still live in traditional mud-and-wood hogans.

The plateau is also the home of the Hopi Tribe, which occupies villages on spectacular mesas. One of the Hopi towns, Old Oraibi, is the oldest continuously occupied settlement in North America. The Hopi people still practice traditional religious ceremonies. The kachina dances take place January through July, and some of them are open to the public.

Lake Powell, one of the most popular attractions in the National Park Service system, draws 3.5 million visitors annually. Often described as "a Grand Canyon with water," Lake Powell is 186 miles long, with 1,960 miles of shoreline. It features orange sandstone cliffs interspersed with sandy beaches and, at 3,700 feet, the area gets sunshine 78 percent of the time. Its prime geological attraction is the world-famous Rainbow Bridge National Monument.

Ruins and artifacts from the Anasazi culture, which thrived in northeast Arizona until about 1,000 years ago, are preserved at Navajo National Monument. Petrified Forest National Park preserves one of the largest exposures of petrified wood in the world. The park's soft, rolling hills of pastel-colored shale positively glow with color just after sunrise or before sunset and are appropriately called the "Painted Desert."

Near Winslow, a giant meteorite smashed into the earth 50,000 years ago, blasting out a crater nearly a mile across. Meteor Crater is one of the best preserved craters on earth and was used by NASA to train lunar astronauts. You can view Meteor Crater from the modern visitor center on its north rim.

For more information:

Holbrook/Petrified Chamber of Commerce
100 E. Arizona St.
Holbrook, AZ 86025
(928) 524-6558; (800) 524-2459
http://holbrookchamberofcommerce.com

Joseph City Chamber of Commerce
(928) 289-2434

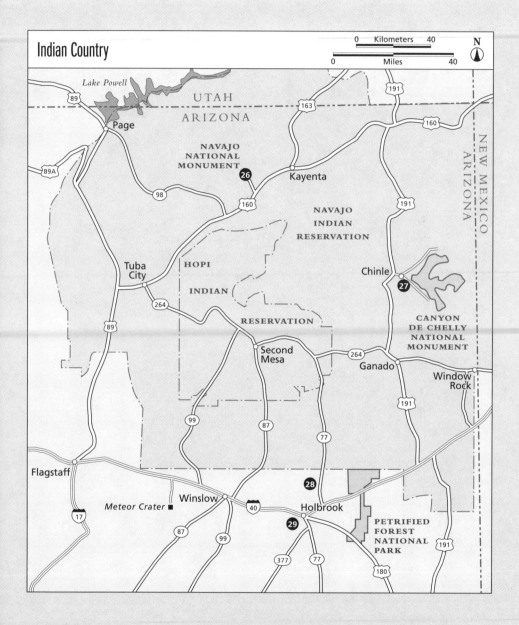

Indian Country

0 Kilometers 40
0 Miles 40

N

UTAH
ARIZONA

Lake Powell

89 Page

89A

NEW MEXICO
ARIZONA

191

163

160

NAVAJO
NATIONAL
MONUMENT 26

Kayenta

98

160

NAVAJO
INDIAN
RESERVATION

191

Tuba
City

HOPI

INDIAN

Chinle

27

264

89

RESERVATION

CANYON
DE CHELLY
NATIONAL
MONUMENT

Second
Mesa

264

Ganado

Window
Rock

191

99

87

77

Flagstaff

17

Meteor Crater ■

Winslow

40

Holbrook

28

29

PETRIFIED
FOREST
NATIONAL
PARK

191

87

99

377

77

180

Mule deer are found from the bottom of the Grand Canyon to the highest mountains in Arizona.

Navajo Nation Tourism Office
PO Box 663
Window Rock, AZ 85615
(928) 871-6436
www.discovernavajo.com

Page/Lake Powell Chamber of Commerce
71 Seventh Ave.
Page, AZ 86040
(928) 645-2741
www.pagechamber.com

Winslow Chamber of Commerce
523 W. Second St.
PO Box 460
Winslow, AZ 86047
(928) 289-2434
www.winslowarizona.org

Number	Name	Elevation	Season	RV/Trailer	Sites	Water	RV dump	Fishing	Hiking trails	Boating	Boat launch	Wheelchair access	Fee	Stay limit, days
26	Betatakin	7,300	May–Oct	•	33		•					•	•	None
27	Cottonwood	5,500	Year-round	•	90	•							•	None
28	Homolovi Ruins	4,850	Year-round	•	53	•	•						•	None
29	Cholla Lake	5,000	Year-round	•	15	•	•	•			•	•	•	None

26 Betatakin

Location: About 40 miles southwest of Kayenta, at Navajo National Monument
Sites: 33 tent and RV to 27 feet; no hookups
Road conditions: Paved
Management: Navajo Parks and Recreation, (928) 674-2106, http://navajonationparks.org
Finding the campground: From Kayenta, drive 29 miles southwest on US 160, and turn right onto AZ 564. (This junction is 54 miles northeast of Tuba City.) Continue 10 miles to the visitor center and campground.
About the campground: The campground is located in a piñon/juniper forest near the rim of Tsegi Canyon. Navajo National Monument, located within the Navajo Indian Reservation, protects a number of ruins that were occupied by the Anasazi people 1,000 years ago. The visitor center is a good place to learn about this tenacious Southwestern culture. This unit of the monument encompasses two of the most famous ruins. Betatakin is visible from a nearby overlook and can be hiked via a 5-mile round-trip. Keet Seel is accessible via a longer trail, which is best done as an overnight hike; access is limited by permit in order to protect the fragile ruins. The nearest services are in Kayenta; full services are available in Page and Flagstaff. Open-flame campfires are not allowed; campers must use stoves.

27 Cottonwood

Location: Near Chinle, at Canyon de Chelly National Monument
Sites: 90 tent and RV up to 34 feet; no hookups
Road conditions: Paved
Management: Canyon de Chelly National Monument, (928) 674-5510, www.nps.gov/cach
Finding the campground: From the junction of US 191 and Tribal Road 64, go 3 miles east on TR 64, through Chinle and past the monument visitor center. Turn right and go 0.5 mile to the campground.
About the campground: Cottonwood campground is a fine base for exploring Canyon del Muerto and Canyon de Chelly, the two beautiful canyons that make up the national monument. Paved roads follow the rims of each canyon. A spectacular foot trail leads to famous White House Ruin.

White House Ruin, Canyon de Chelly

Other canyon-bottom exploration is available on trips with Navajo guides. Group camping is available by reservation. The campground is within walking distance of the cafeteria at Thunderbird Lodge. Contact the park for further information. Limited services are available in Chinle; the nearest full services are in Gallup, New Mexico.

28 Homolovi Ruins

Location: About 6 miles east of Winslow, at Homolovi Ruins State Park
Sites: 53 tent and RV up to 83 feet, with some electric and water hookups
Road conditions: Paved
Management: Homolovi Ruins State Park, (928) 289-4106, azstateparks.com/Parks/HORU; reservations (928) 586-2283, azstateparks.itinio.com/homolovi
Finding the campground: From Winslow, go 4 miles east on I-40; exit at AZ 87. Turn left and continue 1 mile north; turn left and go another mile to the park and campground.
About the campground: This campground is located in the Painted Desert near the ruins of an ancient Native American community. The state park has a visitor center and interpretive trails. World famous for its ethereal beauty, the Painted Desert is gently rolling plateau country. The multiple pastel colors of the exposed shale and sandstone rocks catch the early-morning or late-evening light and provide an ever-changing display of subtle color. Nearby attractions include Meteor Crater, the best preserved impact crater on earth, and Petrified Forest National Park, which protects vast outcrops of fossilized wood. Full services are available in nearby Winslow.

29 Cholla Lake

Location: About 10 miles west of Holbrook
Sites: 15 tent and RV; some partial hookups
Road conditions: Paved
Management: Navajo County Recreation Department, (928) 524-4000, www.navajocountyaz.gov
Finding the campground: From Winslow, go 23 miles east on I-40 (from Holbrook, go 8 miles west on I-40); exit at Joseph City (exit 277). Go south, and then almost immediately turn left (east) onto the park access road; continue 2 miles to the campground.
About the campground: The campground's main attraction is its convenient location near the interstate. Fishing and boating are available on the lake. Nearby attractions include the historic downtown section of Holbrook and Petrified Forest National Park. Full services are available in Holbrook.

River Country

The expansive western deserts and mountains of the state are bordered on the west by the Colorado River, the defining feature of this landscape. A string of dams impound the waters of the river, creating Lake Mead, Lake Mohave, Lake Havasu, and Imperial Reservoir, which provide almost unlimited water recreation. Several national wildlife refuges along the river provide excellent opportunities to observe wildlife. Most of the region's campgrounds are located along the river and its lakes. But don't ignore the desert. There is a great variety of desert backcountry and wilderness to explore. The BLM and the state parks system provide a number of campgrounds, and the sheer vastness of the public lands means you can enjoy dispersed camping in complete solitude if you desire. (Although this FalconGuide covers only the campgrounds on the Arizona side of the river, you will find more facilities and long-term visitor areas on the California side. See FalconGuides' *Camping Southern California* by Richard McMahon, updated by Bruce Grubbs.)

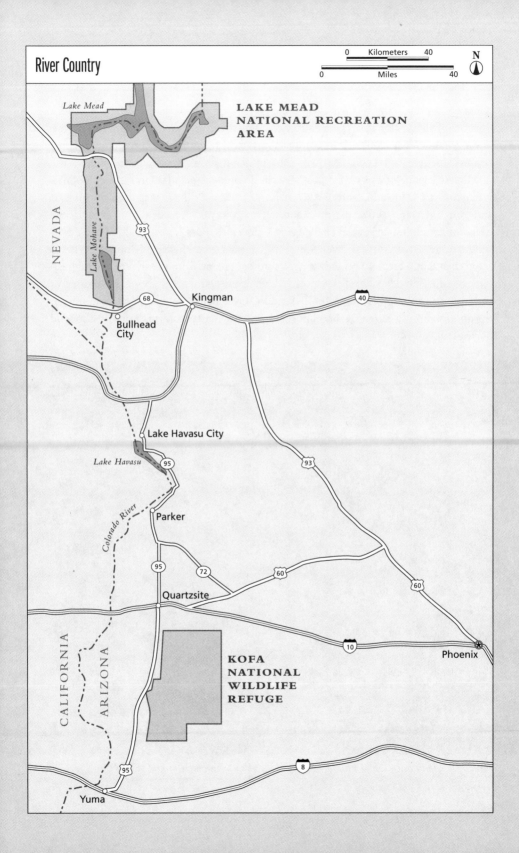

River Country

0 Kilometers 40
0 Miles 40

N

Lake Mead

LAKE MEAD
NATIONAL RECREATION
AREA

NEVADA

Lake Mohave

93

68   Kingman   40

Bullhead
City

Lake Havasu City

Lake Havasu   95

93

Colorado River

Parker

95   72   60

60

Quartzsite

10   Phoenix

CALIFORNIA

ARIZONA

KOFA
NATIONAL
WILDLIFE
REFUGE

95   8

Yuma

Kingman

Kingman, on I-40 and historic Route 66, is the jumping-off point for the northern portion of the Colorado River country. When the river leaves the Grand Canyon at the Grand Wash Cliffs, it's impounded in Lake Mead, the huge reservoir formed behind Hoover Dam. The lake makes a sharp turn from west to south and defines the northwest corner of the state. Lake Mead is an angler's paradise and a very popular water sports playground. Sailing is great fun on the wide-open expanses of the lake, and you can water-ski, scuba dive, and even sea kayak. If you like to explore the backcountry, there are several challenging wilderness areas scattered along the desert mountain ranges east of the river. South of Kingman, the Hualapai Mountains rise to more than 8,000 feet and provide a cool, forested escape from the desert. In Bullhead City, on the Arizona side of the river below Davis Dam, learn about the history of the river and its exploration at the Colorado River Museum. Near Bullhead City is the ghost town of Oatman. Once a busy mining town, Oatman is famous for the wild burros that still wander its streets.

Hualapai Mountains, site of Hualapai Mountain Park Campground and Wild Cow Springs Campground

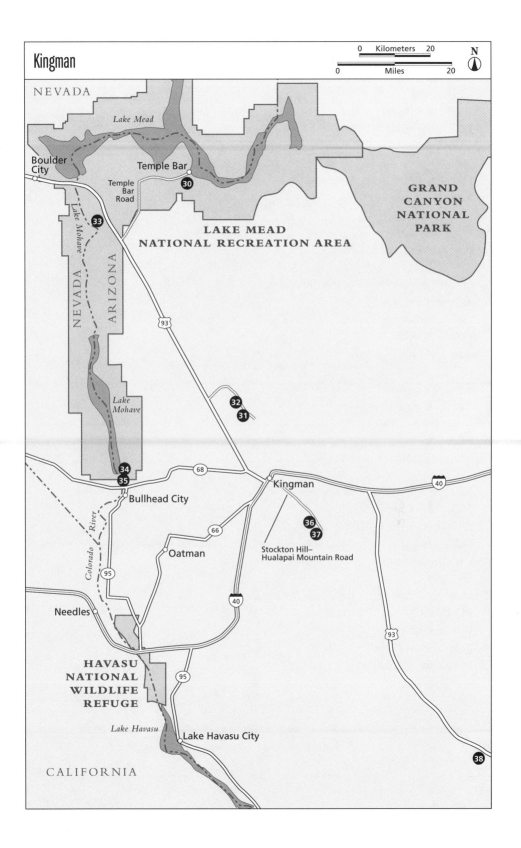

For more information:
Bullhead City Chamber of Commerce
1251 AZ 95
Bullhead City, AZ 86429
(928) 754-4121; (800) 987-7457
www.bullheadchamber.com

Chloride Chamber of Commerce
4940 Tennessee Ave.
Chloride, AZ 86431
(928) 565-2204
www.chloridearizona.com

Dolan Springs Chamber of Commerce
16154 N. Piece Ferry Rd.
Dolan Springs, AZ 86441
(928) 767-4472
www.dolanspringschamberofcommerce.com

Kingman Chamber of Commerce
120 W. Andy Devine Ave.
Kingman, AZ 86401
(928) 753-6253
www.kingmanchamber.org

Mohave Valley Chamber of Commerce
5630 AZ 95, Ste. 5
Ft. Mohave, AZ 86427
(928) 768-2777
www.mohavevalleychamber.org

Oatman Goldroad Chamber of Commerce
PO Box 423
Oatman, AZ 86433
(928) 768-6222
www.oatmangoldroad.org

Number	Name	Elevation	Season	RV/Trailer	Sites	Water	RV dump	Fishing	Hiking trails	Boating	Boat launch	Wheelchair access	Fee	Stay limit, days
30	Temple Bar	1,400	Year-round	•	153	•		•	•	•	•	•	•	30
31	Windy Point	6,000	May–Oct		7				•				•	14
32	Packsaddle	6,000	Year-round		4				•					14
33	Willow Beach	700	Year-round	•	29	•	•	•		•	•	•	•	30
34	Katherine Landing	700	Year-round	•	173	•	•	•		•	•	•	•	30
35	Davis Camp	700	Year-round	•	175	•	•	•		•	•	•	•	None
36	Hualapai Mountain Park	6,200	Year-round	•	70	•			•			•	•	None
37	Wild Cow Springs	6,500	May–Oct	•	24				•			•	•	14
38	Burro Creek	2,000	Year-round	•	30	•				•		•	•	14

30 Temple Bar

Location: About 80 miles north of Kingman, on Lake Mead
Sites: 153 tent and RV; no hookups
Road conditions: Paved
Management: Lake Mead National Recreation Area, (702) 293-8990, www.nps.gov/lame; reservations (928) 767-3211
Finding the campground: From Kingman, go 54 miles north on US 93. Turn right onto Temple Bar Road and continue 26 miles to Temple Bar.
About the campground: The campground is located on Lake Mead in the Mohave Desert. The lake offers fishing for largemouth bass, striped bass, rainbow trout, channel catfish, crappie, and bluegill. Boating, including sailing, kayaking, and canoeing, is popular on the lake. Waterskiing, sailboarding, scuba diving, and snorkeling are also popular. Boat rental and a full-service marina are located in Temple Bar. The nearest full services are in Kingman.

31 Windy Point

Location: About 34 miles north of Kingman, in the Cerbat Mountains
Sites: 7 tent
Road conditions: Paved, dirt
Management: Bureau of Land Management, (928) 718-3700, www.blm.gov/az
Finding the campground: From Kingman, drive 20 miles north on US 93 and turn right onto Big Wash Road. Continue 11 miles east to the campground.
About the campground: This is a small campground set in the rugged Cerbat Mountains, a high-desert range studded with piñon pines and juniper trees. It's a good base for exploring the mountains, including the nearby Mount Tipton Wilderness. The nearest full services are in Kingman.

32 Packsaddle

Location: About 33 miles north of Kingman, in the Cerbat Mountains
Sites: 4 tent
Road conditions: Paved, dirt
Management: Bureau of Land Management, (928) 718-3700, www.blm.gov/az
Finding the campground: From Kingman, drive 20 miles north on US 93, and turn right onto Big Wash Road. Continue 9 miles east to the campground.
About the campground: This is a small tent-only campground in the Cerbat Mountains. Like nearby Windy Point Campground, it's a good base for exploring the mountains. The nearest full services are in Kingman.

33 Willow Beach

Location: About 59 miles northwest of Kingman, on Lake Mohave
Sites: 29 tent and RV up to 25 feet; full hookups
Road conditions: Paved
Management: Lake Mead National Recreation Area, (702) 293-8990, www.nps.gov/lame; reservations (928) 767-4747
Finding the campground: From Kingman, go north 55.6 miles on US 93. Turn left at the signed turnoff for Willow Beach, and continue 2.5 miles.
About the campground: This small campground is in the Mohave Desert on the east shore of 67-mile-long Lake Mohave. Lake Mohave offers a wide range of boating and water sports and is fished for trout, catfish, and striped, largemouth, and smallmouth bass. A full-service marina is available, and full services are available in Kingman and Bullhead City.

34 Katherine Landing

Location: About 34 miles west of Kingman, on Lake Mohave
Sites: 173 tent and RV up to 25 feet; no hookups
Road conditions: Paved
Management: Lake Mead National Recreation Area, (702) 293-8990, www.nps.gov/lame; reservations (928) 754-3245
Finding the campground: From Bullhead City at the junction of AZ 95 and AZ 68, go north about 3 miles on AZ 68. Turn left onto the park access road, and go north 3 miles to the campground. This turnoff is 30 miles west of Kingman.
About the campground: This large campground is in the Mohave Desert on the southeast shore of 67-mile-long Lake Mohave. Lake Mohave offers a wide range of boating and water sports and is fished for trout, catfish, and striped, largemouth, and smallmouth bass. A full-service marina is available, and full services are available in Bullhead City.

35 Davis Camp

Location: Bullhead City, on the Colorado River
Sites: 175 tent and RV; full hookups
Road conditions: Paved
Management: Mohave County Parks, (928) 754-7250, www.mcparks.com/davis_camp.htm
Finding the campground: From Bullhead City, go north on AZ 95 to the park entrance road.
About the campground: This is a desert campground on the Colorado River below Davis Dam. Hookups are available, as are showers. The river is fished for largemouth and smallmouth bass, as well as other species. Full services are available in Bullhead City.

36 Hualapai Mountain Park

Location: About 13 miles southeast of Kingman, in the Hualapai Mountains
Sites: 70 tent and RV; some hookups available
Road conditions: Paved
Management: Hualapai Mountain Park, (928) 681-5700, www.mcparks.com/hualapai_mt_park.htm
Finding the campground: From Kingman, go 13 miles southeast on Stockton Hill–Hualapai Mountain Road to the park.
About the campground: The campground and park is located in granite and pine country in the Hualapai Mountains, high above the hot Mohave Desert. The Hualapai Mountain Trail is popular with hikers, and there are several other trails nearby. Backcountry hikers can explore the nearby Wabayuma Peak Wilderness, which is farther south along the crest. Full services are available in Kingman.

Aspen Peak in the Hualapai Mountains

37 Wild Cow Springs

Location: About 19 miles southeast of Kingman, in the Hualapai Mountains
Sites: 24 tent and RV; no hookups
Road conditions: Paved, dirt
Management: Bureau of Land Management, (928) 718-3700, www.blm.gov/az
Finding the campground: From Kingman, go 14 miles southeast on Stockton Hill–Hualapai Mountain Road. Continue 5 miles on Hualapai Ridge Road.
About the campground: This campground is located high in the rugged Hualapai Mountains, a pine-forested island surrounded by the Mohave Desert. It's not only a good escape from the hot desert but also a starting point for exploring the mountains, including Wayabuma Peak Wilderness to the south. There are several hiking trails in the Hualapai Peak and Wabayuma Peak areas. Full services are available in Kingman.

38 Burro Creek

Location: About 68 miles southeast of Kingman, on Burro Creek
Sites: 30 tent and RV; no hookups
Road conditions: Paved
Management: Bureau of Land Management, (928) 718-3700, www.blm.gov/az
Finding the campground: From Kingman, go 22 miles east on I-40 and turn south onto US 93. Continue 46 miles to the campground, which is on the right.
About the campground: This desert campground is a popular winter spot, but it's a bit hot in summer. It's a good base for exploring several nearby backcountry areas, including Burro Creek, Arrastra Mountain, and Aubrey Peak Wildernesses. Full services are available in Kingman and Wickenburg.

Lake Havasu

Lake Havasu is famous as the site of London Bridge, but there's more to this central section of the River Country than transplanted bridges. The upper end of the lake is contained in Havasu National Wildlife Refuge, a haven for waterfowl and a paddler's paradise. Boaters, sailors, and other water sports enthusiasts and anglers all enjoy the impounded waters of the lake, formed by Parker Dam. There are campgrounds along the lakeshore and the river, above and below the dam. A tributary of the Colorado, the Bill Williams River has been dammed to create Alamo Reservoir. The state park here is a good jumping-off point for exploring the nearby desert wilderness areas. Cultural attractions include the Creative Cultural Center in Lake Havasu City, where year-round events feature Native American and Southwestern arts and crafts, traditional dancing, and storytelling. You can also visit the tribal museum on the Colorado River Indian Reservation, just south of Parker. It represents the Navajo, Hopi, Mohave, and Chemehuevi Tribes.

Sea kayaking on Lake Havasu

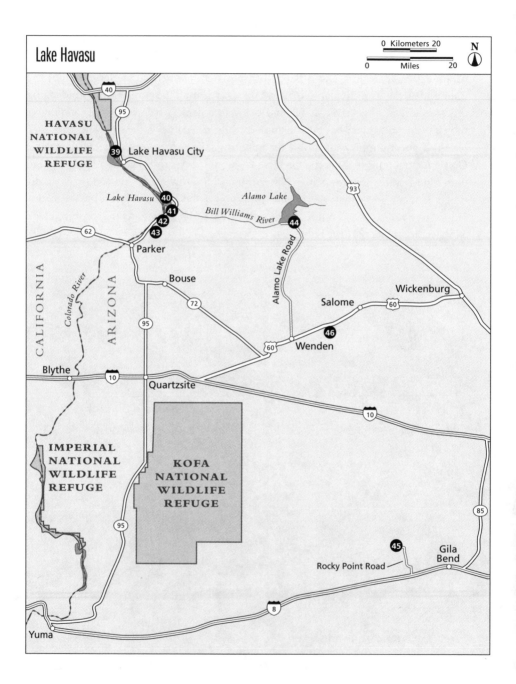

Lake Havasu

The southern section of River Country is anchored by the sunny city of Yuma. Located near the Mexican border in the lowest part of the state, Yuma offers warm winters and desert hiking as well as opportunities for water sports and fishing. Cultural attractions include a number of museums and Yuma Territorial Prison State Historic Park. Inland, the desert town of Quartzite is a winter mecca for RVers escaping colder climates and for rockhounds who are attracted to the gem and mineral shows. The Kofa National Wildlife Refuge is a preserve established to protect the majestic desert bighorn sheep and is an interesting and challenging wilderness to explore. In the Kofa Mountains, Palm Canyon is the site of the only native palm trees in Arizona.

There are few public campgrounds, but the BLM has designated several long-term visitor areas in the desert, so there are plenty of places to camp. If you want to escape the crowds, dispersed camping is allowed on most of the public land in southwest Arizona.

For more information:
Bouse Chamber of Commerce
44362 E. Main St.
PO Box 817
Bouse, AZ 85325
(928) 851-2509
www.bousechamber.org

Ehrenberg Chamber of Commerce
PO Box 800
Ehrenberg, AZ 85334
(928) 923-9661
www.coloradoriverinfo.com/ehrenberg/chamber

Gila Bend Chamber of Commerce
PO Box CC
Gila Bend, AZ 85337
(928) 420-1964
www.gilabendazchamber.com

Lake Havasu Chamber of Commerce
314 London Bridge Rd.
Lake Havasu City, AZ 86403
(928) 855-4115
www.havasuchamber.com

McMullen Valley Chamber of Commerce
PO Box 700
Salome, AZ 85348
(928) 859-3846
www.azoutback.com/mcmullen.htm

Parker Area Chamber of Commerce
1217 California Ave.
Parker, AZ 85344
(928) 669-2174
www.parkeraz.org

Quartzsite Chamber of Commerce
101 W. Main St.
PO Box 2566
Quartzsite, AZ 85346
(928) 927-9321
www.quartzsitebusinesschamber.com

Somerton Chamber of Commerce
PO Box 638
Somerton, AZ 85350
(928) 627-8866
www.somertonchamber.com

Welton Chamber of Commerce
PO Box 67
Welton, AZ 85356
(928) 785-3348

Yuma Convention and Visitors Bureau and Chamber of Commerce
180 W. First St., Ste. A
Yuma, AZ 85364
(800) 782-2567
www.yumachamber.org

Number	Name	Elevation	Season	RV/Trailer	Sites	Water	RV dump	Fishing	Hiking trails	Boating	Boat launch	Wheelchair access	Fee	Stay limit, days
39	Lake Havasu	450	Year-round	•	42	•	•	•	•	•	•	•	•	14
40	Cattail Cove	480	Year-round	•	61	•	•	•	•	•	•	•	•	14
41	River Island	420	Year-round		37	•		•			•	•	•	14
42	Buckskin Mountain	420	Year-round	•	68	•	•	•	•	•	•	•	•	14
43	La Paz County Park	400	Year-round	•	114	•	•	•	•			•	•	14
44	Alamo Lake State Park	1,250	Year-round	•	394	•	•	•	•	•	•	•	•	14
45	Painted Rock Petroglyph	800	Year-round	•	30									14
46	Centennial County Park	1,830	Year-round	•	26	•	•	•					•	14

39 Lake Havasu

Location: Lake Havasu City, on Lake Havasu
Sites: 42 tent and RV; no hookups
Road conditions: Paved
Management: Lake Havasu State Park, (928) 855-2784, azstateparks.com/Parks/LAHA; reservations (520) 586-2283
Finding the campground: The park is just north of London Bridge off London Bridge Road.
About the campground: This state park on Windsor Beach is a popular water sports destination. The lake is fished for striped bass, largemouth bass, and carp. Showers are available. A group campsite is available by reservation. The campground is also a good base for exploring the Havasu Wilderness and the Needles area to the north. Full services are available in Lake Havasu City.

40 Cattail Cove

Location: About 10 miles south of Lake Havasu City, on Lake Havasu
Sites: 61 tent and RV; water and electric hookups
Road conditions: Paved
Management: Cattail Cove State Park, (928) 855-1223, azstateparks.com/Parks/CACO; reservations (520) 586-2283
Finding the campground: From Lake Havasu City, drive south about 10 miles on AZ 95; turn right into the park.
About the campground: Another lakeside campground, this site features boat-only campsites in addition to auto campsites. Showers are available. Limited supplies are available near the park, with full services in Lake Havasu City.

41 River Island

Location: About 10 miles south of Lake Havasu City, on Lake Havasu
Sites: 37 tent; no hookups
Road conditions: Paved
Management: River Island State Park, (928) 667-3386, azstateparks.com/Parks/RIIS; reservations (520) 586-2283
Finding the campground: From Lake Havasu City, drive south about 9 miles on AZ 95; turn right into the park.
About the campground: This is a tent-only campground located on the shore of Lake Havasu in a rugged mountain setting. Limited supplies are available near the park, with full services in Lake Havasu City.

42 Buckskin Mountain

Location: About 11 miles northeast of Parker, on the Colorado River
Sites: 68 tent and RV; some hookups
Road conditions: Paved
Management: Buckskin Mountain State Park, (928) 667-3231, www.pr.state.us/parks/parkhtml/buckskin.html; reservations (520) 586-2283
Finding the campground: From Parker, go north about 11 miles on AZ 95 to the park turnoff.
About the campground: This riverside campground has showers, grass, and shade trees. There are several scenic hiking trails. The river is fished for largemouth and striped bass, as well as crappie, sunfish, and channel catfish. Limited services are available nearby; full services are available in Parker.

43 La Paz County Park

Location: About 8 miles northeast of Parker, on the Colorado River
Sites: 114 tent and RV; water, electric, and cable TV hookups
Road conditions: Paved
Management: La Paz County Parks, (928) 667-2069, www.co.la-paz.az.us
Finding the campground: From Parker, go about 8 miles north on AZ 95; then left into the campground.
About the campground: This section of the river is a prime spot for waterskiing. Some sites have hookups and sun shelters, and there are beach campsites. Limited services are available nearby; full services are available in Parker.

Teddy bear cholla looks cuddly but beware the needle-sharp barbed spines.

44 Alamo Lake State Park

Location: About 86 miles northwest of Wickenburg, at Alamo Lake
Sites: 394 tent and RV; some electric hookups
Road conditions: Paved
Management: Alamo Lake State Park, (928) 669-2088, azstateparks.com/Parks/ALLA; reservations (520) 586-2283
Finding the campground: From Wickenburg, go 52 miles west on US 60 to Wenden and turn right (north) onto Alamo Lake Road. Continue 34 miles north to the park.
About the campground: An out-of-the-way but popular area, Alamo Lake is a flood-control basin. The lake is fished for largemouth bass, channel and flathead catfish, tilapia, bullhead, carp, and sunfish. Some campsites have hookups; showers are available, as is a group camp area. Limited services are available in Wenden; full services are available in Parker and Wickenburg.

45 Painted Rock Petroglyph

Location: About 31 miles northwest of Gila Bend
Sites: 30 tent and RV; no hookups
Road conditions: Dirt
Management: Bureau of Land Management, (623) 580-5500, www.blm.gov/az/st/en/prog/recreation/camping/dev_camps/painted_rock.html
Finding the campground: From Gila Bend, go about 16 miles west on I-8 to the Painted Rock interchange, and then north 15 miles on Rocky Point Road.
About the campground: The campground is in the desert near Painted Rock Reservoir, a flood-control basin on the Gila River. The rugged Gila Bend Mountains, which include the Woolsey Peak and Signal Peak Wildernesses, lie to the north. The campground's main feature is Hohokam rock art. The historic Mormon Battalion Trail and the Butterfield Stage Route pass through this area. The nearest full services are in Gila Bend.

46 Centennial County Park

Location: Near Wenden, south of US 60
Sites: 26 tent and RV; no hookups
Road conditions: Paved
Management: La Paz County Parks, (928) 667-2069, www.co.la-paz.az.us
Finding the campground: From Wenden on US 60, drive east 1 mile. Turn right (south) onto Centennial Park Road, and drive 2 miles to the park and campground.
About the campground: Located in the McMullen Valley, this campground is a good base for exploring the nearby Harcuvar and Harquahala Mountains, as well as surrounding desert areas.

Central Territory

C entral Arizona is a land of rugged, pine-forested mountains with a colorful history. The city of Prescott was the territorial capital before Arizona became a state in 1912, and it still has a flavor of those days. Nearby, the Bradshaw Mountains were a major mining center and the site of several large boomtowns. The winding Senator Highway, a dirt road, runs the length of the Bradshaws. Still interesting to explore today, a hundred years ago it was the main road connecting Arizona Territory's two major cities, Prescott and Tucson. To get a feel for the pioneer days, check out Prescott's Courthouse Plaza and Whiskey Row.

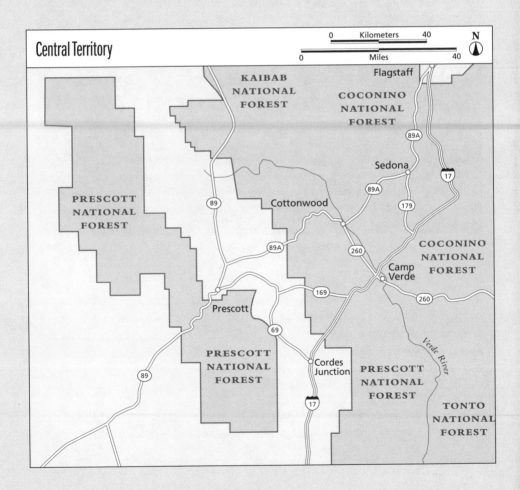

Indian Paintbrush has a long flowering season during spring and summer in Arizona's Central Mountains

Southwest of Prescott, Wickenburg also has managed to preserve a flavor of the old days. Named for a prosperous gold miner, Wickenburg has long been known for its guest ranches, which vary from simple and plain to truly elegant. Check out the Desert Caballeros Western Museum, which features cowboy art and displays about Native Americans and pioneer life.

Prescott

There are plenty of outdoor activities in the Prescott area. Several small lakes attract anglers, and Granite Mountain offers world-class rock climbing. Mountain bikers can explore miles of forest roads and trails. Hikers have several wilderness areas to visit, including Juniper Mesa, Apache Creek, Granite Mountain, Woodchute, and Castle Creek Wildernesses.

For more information:
Arizona Highway 69 Chamber of Commerce
12791 E. Central Ave., Ste. B
Mayer, AZ 86333
(928) 632-4355
www.arizonahighway69chamber.org

Black Canyon City Chamber of Commerce
PO Box 1919
Black Canyon City, AZ 853224
(623) 374-9797
blackcanyonaz.com/community.html

Chino Valley Chamber of Commerce
175 E. Road 2 South
Chino Valley, AZ 86323
(928) 636-2493
www.chinovalley.org

Prescott Chamber of Commerce
117 W. Goodwin St.
Prescott, AZ 86302
(928) 445-2000; (800) 266-7534
www.prescott.org

Prescott Valley Chamber of Commerce
3001 N. Main St., Ste. 2A
Prescott Valley, AZ 86314
(928) 772-8857
www.pvchamber.org

Wickenburg Chamber of Commerce
216 N. Frontier St.
Wickenburg, AZ 85390
(928) 684-5479
www.wickenburgchamber.com

Little Granite Mountain Trail

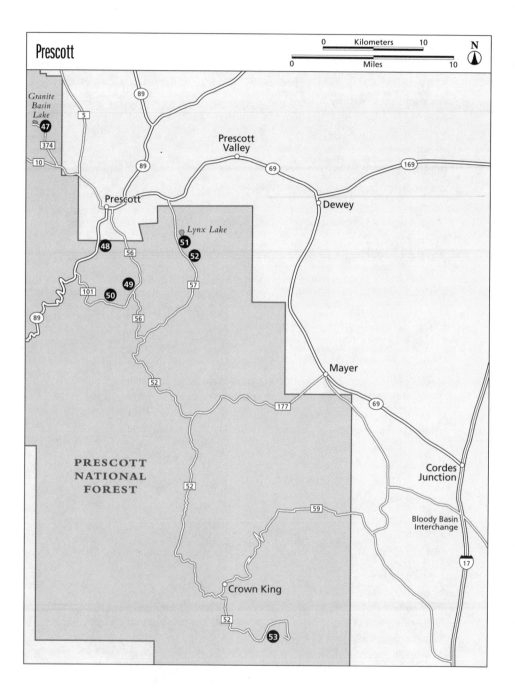

Prescott

Granite
Basin
Lake
47

374

5

89

89

10

Prescott

Prescott
Valley

69

169

Dewey

Lynx Lake
51

48

56

52

49

101

50

57

56

89

52

177

Mayer

69

PRESCOTT
NATIONAL
FOREST

52

59

Cordes
Junction

Bloody Basin
Interchange

17

52

Crown King

52

53

Number	Name	Elevation	Season	RV/Trailer	Sites	Water	RV dump	Fishing	Hiking trails	Boating	Boat launch	Wheelchair access	Fee	Stay limit, days
47	Yavapai	5,600	Year-round	•	21	•			•			•	•	14
48	White Spar	5,700	Year-round	•	57	•						•	•	14
49	Groom Creek Horse Camp	6,000	May–Oct	•	36	•	•					•	•	14
50	Lower Wolf Creek	6,000	May–Nov	•	20				•				•	14
51	Lynx Lake	5,600	Apr–Nov	•	36	•	•	•	•	•			•	7
52	Hilltop	5,700	Apr–Oct	•	38	•		•	•				•	7
53	Hazlett Hollow	6,000	May–Oct	•	15	•		•	•			•	•	14

47 Yavapai

Location: About 8 miles northwest of Prescott, near Granite Mountain
Sites: 21 tent and RV up to 40 feet; no hookups
Road conditions: Paved
Management: Prescott National Forest, (928) 443-8000, www.fs.usda.gov/prescott
Finding the campground: From Prescott, drive west about 4 miles on Iron Springs Road, FR 10. Turn right onto Granite Basin Road, FR 374, and continue 2 miles to the campground.
About the campground: Located near the popular Granite Basin Recreation Area, this campground makes a fine base for exploring Granite Mountain Wilderness. Several hiking trails lead into the wilderness and surrounding country and to the top of Granite Mountain Wall, which is famous for its world-class rock climbing. The historical attractions in Prescott are also close at hand. Full services are available in Prescott.

48 White Spar

Location: About 3 miles southwest of Prescott, in the Bradshaw Mountains
Sites: 57 tent and RV up to 32 feet; no hookups
Road conditions: Paved, dirt
Management: Prescott National Forest, (928) 443-8000, www.fs.usda.gov/prescott
Finding the campground: From Prescott, drive about 3 miles south on AZ 89.
About the campground: This popular, pine-forested campground is very convenient to Prescott and makes a good starting point for exploring the nearby Bradshaw Mountains and Sierra Prieta. The Sharlot Hall Museum in Prescott is a good place to get a feel for life in nineteenth-century territorial Arizona, when Prescott was the capital. Full services are available in Prescott.

Granite Mountain Wall is a world-class rock climbing area.

49 Groom Creek Horse Camp

Location: 9 miles south of Prescott, in the Bradshaw Mountains
Sites: 36 tent and RV up to 35 feet; no hookups
Road conditions: Paved
Management: Prescott National Forest, (928) 443-8000, www.fs.usda.gov/prescott; reservations (928) 443-8000
Finding the campground: From Prescott, drive 9 miles south on FR 56.
About the campground: This is an equestrian camp, and there are several popular horse trails in the nearby forest. The nearest services are in Prescott.

50 Lower Wolf Creek

Location: About 12 miles south of Prescott, in the Bradshaw Mountains
Sites: 20 tent and RV up to 32 feet; no hookups
Road conditions: Paved, dirt
Management: Prescott National Forest, (928) 443-8000, www.fs.usda.gov/prescott
Finding the campground: From Prescott, drive about 10 miles south on FR 56. Turn right onto FR 101 and continue about 2 miles to the campground.
About the campground: This is another out-of-the-way campground that makes a good base for exploring the Bradshaw Mountains. There are numerous hiking trails and back roads for mountain bikers and four-wheelers to explore. Full services are available in Prescott.

51 Lynx Lake

Location: About 5 miles southeast of Prescott, in the Bradshaw Mountains
Sites: 36 tent and RV up to 32 feet; no hookups
Road conditions: Paved
Management: Prescott National Forest, (928) 443-8000, www.fs.usda.gov/prescott
Finding the campground: From Prescott, drive about 3 miles east on AZ 69. Turn right onto Walker Road, FR 57, and continue 2 miles to the campground.
About the campground: With scenic Lynx Lake as a backdrop, this forested campground is one of the nicest in central Arizona. Walker Road continues into the northern Bradshaw Mountains, which you can explore by vehicle or mountain bike. Fishing is very popular here, as is boating (limited to 1 hp electric motors). The nearest services are in Prescott.

52 Hilltop

Location: 6 miles southeast of Prescott, in the Bradshaw Mountains
Sites: 38 tent and RV up to 32 feet; no hookups
Road conditions: Paved
Management: Prescott National Forest, (928) 443-8000, www.fs.usda.gov/prescott
Finding the campground: From Prescott, drive about 3 miles east on AZ 69. Turn right onto Walker Road, FR 57, and continue 3 miles to the campground.
About the campground: The second campground at Lynx Lake. Prescott has the nearest services.

53 Hazlett Hollow

Location: About 7 miles southeast of Crown King, in the Bradshaw Mountains
Sites: 15 tent and RV up to 32 feet; no hookups
Road conditions: Dirt
Management: Prescott National Forest, (928) 443-8000, www.fs.usda.gov/prescott
Finding the campground: From I-17 at the junction with AZ 69, go south on I-17 for 3 miles to the Bloody Basin interchange. Turn right (west) onto the Crown King Road; go 3 miles, and then turn left at Crown King. After another 3 miles, turn right onto Crown King Road, FR 59. Continue 16 miles, just past the town of Crown King, and turn left on FR 52. Continue another 7 miles to the campground.
About the campground: Located in scenic Horsethief Basin, this camp is a good base for exploring the nearby Castle Creek Wilderness. There are a number of hiking trails both inside and outside the wilderness. Limited fishing and boating is available on Horsethief Lake. The nearest services are in Crown King; the nearest full services are in Prescott.

Verde Valley

Named by Spanish explorers in the 1540s, the Verde Valley's defining natural feature is the Verde River. Native Americans thrived in the area long before the Europeans arrived, as evidenced by numerous ruins. Two outstanding examples are preserved as national monuments. Tuzigoot National Monument features a hilltop dwelling of many rooms; Montezuma Castle National Monument protects a multistory cliff dwelling. Artifacts in these dwellings prove that trade was carried on with peoples from as far away as southern Mexico. There are many other ruins that can be reached by vehicle or foot.

Jerome, on the steep slopes of Mingus Mountain, was the site of one of the richest copper mines in the world. When the mines played out, Jerome nearly became a ghost town. It has since enjoyed a steady revival as an art colony. You can explore the fascinating history of the area at Jerome State Historic Park. Mingus Mountain offers campgrounds in the cool pines at nearly 8,000 feet and some very scenic hiking trails.

The largest town in the Verde Valley is Cottonwood, a thriving retirement community. Nearby Clarkdale is the terminus for the scenic Verde River Railroad and

Camping in the Red Rocks, Sedona

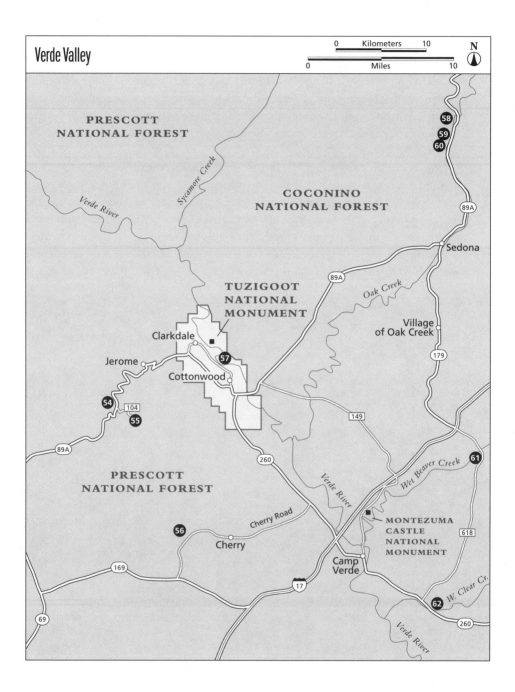

Verde Valley

0 Kilometers 10
0 Miles 10

N

PRESCOTT
NATIONAL FOREST

Sycamore Creek

Verde River

COCONINO
NATIONAL FOREST

58
59
60

89A

Sedona

TUZIGOOT
NATIONAL
MONUMENT

89A

Oak Creek

Clarkdale

Village
of Oak Creek

Jerome

179

Cottonwood

57

54
104
55

149

89A

260

PRESCOTT
NATIONAL FOREST

Verde River

Wet Beaver Creek

61

56

Cherry Road

MONTEZUMA
CASTLE
NATIONAL
MONUMENT

618

Cherry

169

Camp
Verde

W. Clear Cr.

69

17

62

260

Verde River

also the jumping-off point for hikers wanting to investigate the Sycamore Canyon Wilderness. At the lower end of the Verde Valley, the small town of Camp Verde was once a bustling and important military post. Fort Verde State Historic Park preserves some of the original buildings that US Army personnel used during the Apache Indian wars. Camp Verde is also the launching point for float trips down the wilderness section of the Verde River.

Snuggled under the red rocks of the Mogollon Rim at the northeast corner of the Verde Valley, Sedona offers numerous art galleries and other Southwestern shopping experiences. Sedona is surrounded by national forest and wilderness areas containing some of the most dramatic landscapes in Arizona. One of the most famous is Oak Creek Canyon, which features a rare but accessible permanent stream. You can fish the creek or hike some of the many trails found along the canyon's length, using any of several campgrounds as a base. There are also picnic areas for day use. Other hiking trails penetrate the Red Rock–Secret Mountain, Munds Mountain, Wet Beaver Creek, and Clear Creek Wildernesses. Mountain bikers can explore miles of trails on public land outside the wildernesses.

For more information:
Camp Verde Chamber of Commerce
385 S. Main St.
Camp Verde, AZ 86322
(928) 567-9294
www.visitcampverde.com

Cottonwood Chamber of Commerce
1010 S. Main St.
Cottonwood, AZ 86326
(928) 634-7593
www.cottonwoodchamberaz.org

Jerome Chamber of Commerce
PO Box K
Jerome, AZ 86331
(928) 634-2900
www.jeromechamber.com

Number	Name	Elevation	Season	RV/Trailer	Sites	Water	RV dump	Fishing	Hiking trails	Boating	Boat launch	Wheelchair access	Fee	Stay limit, days
54	Potato Patch	7,000	May–Oct	•	24	•		•				•	•	14
55	Mingus Mountain	7,600	May–Oct	•	24			•					•	14
56	Powell Springs	5,300	Year-round	•	11								•	14
57	Dead Horse Ranch	3,300	Year-round	•	100	•	•	•	•	•	•	•	•	14
58	Pine Flat	5,500	Apr–Oct	•	56	•		•	•			•	•	7
59	Cave Springs	5,400	Apr–Oct	•	82	•	•	•	•			•	•	7
60	Manzanita	4,800	Year-round		18	•		•	•			•	•	7
61	Beaver Creek	3,800	Year-round	•	13	•		•	•				•	7
62	Clear Creek	3,200	Year-round	•	18	•		•					•	7

54 Potato Patch

Location: About 23 miles northeast of Prescott, on Woodchute Mountain
Sites: 24 tent and RV up to 22 feet; no hookups
Road conditions: Paved
Management: Prescott National Forest, (928) 443-8000, www.fs.usda.gov/prescott
Finding the campground: From Prescott, drive about 5 miles north on AZ 89 and turn right (east) onto AZ 89A. Drive about 18 miles to the pass on Mingus Mountain and turn left into the campground.
About the campground: Located in a pine-forested hollow on the southeast corner of the mesa-like top of Woodchute Mountain, this campground is a good base for exploring the trails in the Woodchute Wilderness. Nearby Jerome was once a busy copper-mining town and is now an artists' colony and popular tourist destination. You can learn about the history of the area at Jerome State Historic Park, located in a former mansion. The nearest services are in Jerome; full services are in Prescott and Cottonwood.

55 Mingus Mountain

Location: About 26 miles northeast of Prescott, on Mingus Mountain
Sites: 24 tent and RV up to 22 feet; no hookups
Road conditions: Paved, dirt
Management: Prescott National Forest, (928) 443-8000, www.fs.usda.gov/prescott
Finding the campground: From Prescott, drive about 5 miles north on AZ 89 and turn right (east) onto AZ 89A. Drive about 18 miles to the pass on Mingus Mountain. Turn right (south) onto FR 104 and go about 3 miles to the campground.

The view from Mingus Mountain encompasses the Sedona Red Rock area and the Mogollon Rim.

About the campground: The campground is on the ponderosa pine–forested summit plateau of Mingus Mountain. There are spectacular views of central Arizona from the nearby rim and a network of hiking trails leading off the rim. Group camping is available at nearby Playground Campground. The nearest services are in Jerome; full services are in Prescott and Cottonwood.

56 Powell Springs

Location: About 28 miles east of Prescott, in the Black Hills
Sites: 11 tent and RV up to 16 feet; no hookups
Road conditions: Paved, all-weather dirt
Management: Prescott National Forest, (928) 443-8000, www.fs.usda.gov/prescott
Finding the campground: From Prescott, drive about 14 miles south on AZ 69, and turn left (east) onto AZ 169. Continue about 9 miles; turn left (north) onto Cherry Road, FR 75, and go about 5 miles to the campground.
About the campground: This small, out-of-the-way campground is tucked into the rugged Black Hills south of Mingus Mountain. You could use this campground as a base for mountain biking and exploring the Black Hills. The Pine Mountain and Cedar Mesa Wildernesses, southeast along the Verde Rim, have trails for backcountry hikers. The nearest services are in Dewey and Camp Verde.

57 Dead Horse Ranch

Location: Cottonwood, in the Verde Valley
Sites: 100 tent and RV; water and electric hookups
Road conditions: Paved
Management: Dead Horse State Park, (928) 634-5283, azstateparks.com/Parks/DEHO; reservations (520) 586-2283
Finding the campground: From Main Street in Cottonwood, turn north on 10th Street, go 0.1 mile, and turn right into the park.
About the campground: The park features a nature trail and fishing. Showers and partial hookups are available, along with group camping by reservation. Full services are available in Cottonwood. Nearby attractions include the historic mining town of Jerome and Tuzigoot National Monument, as well as the Verde Canyon Scenic Railroad.

58 Pine Flat

Location: About 12 miles north of Sedona, in Oak Creek Canyon
Sites: 56 tent and RV up to 32 feet; no hookups
Road conditions: Paved
Management: Coconino National Forest, (928) 527-3620, www.fs.usda.gov/main/coconino/home; reservations (877) 444-6777, www.recreation.gov

Finding the campground: From Sedona, drive 12 miles north on AZ 89A. The campground is on both sides of the highway.

About the campground: The campground is in the cool depths of Oak Creek Canyon in a shady stand of ponderosa pines. Oak Creek, which is fished for trout, is next to the campground. A trail climbs to the east rim of the canyon for spectacular views of the upper canyon. Like all Oak Creek campgrounds, Pine Flat fills early on weekends and holidays. There are limited services in Oak Creek Canyon; the nearest full services are in Sedona.

59 Cave Springs

Location: About 10 miles north of Sedona, in Oak Creek Canyon
Sites: 82 tent and RV up to 32 feet; no hookups
Road conditions: Paved
Management: Coconino National Forest, (928) 527-3620, www.fs.usda.gov/main/coconino/home; reservations (877) 444-6777, www.recreation.gov
Finding the campground: From Sedona, drive 10 miles north on AZ 89A; turn left into the campground.
About the campground: The largest campground in Oak Creek Canyon, it is also located farther from the highway than the others, which means you'll hear more of the creek and less of the traffic. It makes a fine base for exploring Oak Creek and its attractions, such as trout fishing and hiking. The canyon floor is forested with ponderosa pine. Deciduous trees, such as Arizona sycamore and Fremont cottonwood, surround Oak Creek, which flows past the edge of the campground. These trees and others create a fine display of fall color in October. Like all Oak Creek campgrounds, Cave Spring fills early on weekends and holidays. There are limited services in Oak Creek Canyon; the nearest full services are in Sedona.

60 Manzanita

Location: About 6 miles north of Sedona, in Oak Creek Canyon
Sites: 18 tent
Road conditions: Paved
Management: Coconino National Forest, (928) 527-3620, www.fs.usda.gov/main/coconino/home; reservations (877) 444-6777, www.recreation.gov
Finding the campground: From Sedona, drive 6 miles north on AZ 89A; turn left into the campground.
About the campground: This is the closest campground to Sedona. Like all Oak Creek campgrounds, Manzanita fills early on weekends and holidays. Trout fishing is popular in the creek, and there are several hiking trails nearby. The North Wilson Trail is an ambitious hike to the top of Wilson Mountain, while the Sterling Pass Trail follows an old Indian route to Sterling Canyon. There are limited services in Oak Creek Canyon; the nearest full services are in Sedona.

61 Beaver Creek

Location: About 17 miles southeast of Sedona, on Wet Beaver Creek
Sites: 13 tent and RV up to 22 feet; no hookups
Road conditions: Paved
Management: Coconino National Forest, (928) 527-3620, www.fs.usda.gov/main/coconino/home; reservations (877) 444-6777, www.recreation.gov
Finding the campground: From Sedona, go 14 miles south on AZ 179. Cross under I-17 and continue 2.5 miles on FR 618 to the campground. From I-17, take the Sedona exit. Turn right onto FR 618.
About the campground: This small campground is near an interstate but still feels out of the way. It's located on the banks of Wet Beaver Creek, a permanent stream flowing from beneath the Mogollon Rim. The streamside riparian forest of Arizona sycamores and Fremont cottonwoods provides shade. Hiking is available on the nearby Apache Maid Trail, which follows the creek upstream, and in West Clear Creek, which is farther south on FR 618. Other nearby attractions include Montezuma Well and Montezuma Castle National Monuments, which preserve unique ruins left by the people who lived in the area 1,000 years ago. The nearest services are in Camp Verde; full services are available in Cottonwood.

62 Clear Creek

Location: About 3 miles southeast of Camp Verde, on West Clear Creek
Sites: 18 tent and RV up to 32 feet; no hookups
Road conditions: Paved, all-weather dirt
Management: Coconino National Forest, (928) 527-3620, www.fs.usda.gov/main/coconino/home
Finding the campground: From Camp Verde, drive 8 miles east on AZ 260 to the campground, which is on the left.
About the campground: The campground is on West Clear Creek, a cold, permanent creek flowing from a deep canyon in the Mogollon Rim. The creek is popular with anglers and wildlife watchers. Though the campground is in desert grassland, shade is provided by the streamside Fremont cottonwoods. Group camping is available. Nearby attractions include Montezuma Well and Montezuma Castle National Monuments and Fort Verde State Park. The nearest services are in Camp Verde; full services are available in Cottonwood.

West Clear Creek tumbles through a deep canyon below the Mogollon Rim.

Valley of the Sun

Phoenix and its sister cities in the Valley of the Sun are home to more than five million people, well over half the state's population. With such an urban concentration, it's hard to believe there are public campgrounds within easy reach of the city. However, the desert valley lies on the edge of the rugged central mountains and is bordered on the north and east by the 2.9-million-acre Tonto National Forest, the largest in the country. In addition, several regional county parks have campgrounds. You can ride a bike or hike on trails in most of the regional parks, and miles of back roads and trails are open to mountain bikers in the national

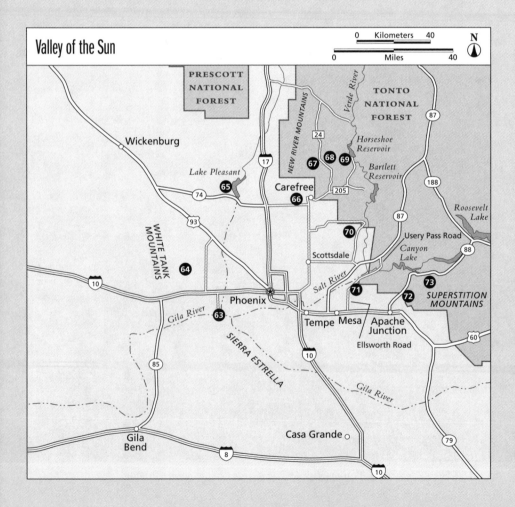

Valley of the Sun

Kilometers 0 ———— 40

Miles 0 ———— 40

N

forest. Backcountry hikers can find complete solitude in the Four Peaks and Superstition Wildernesses. Boaters, water sports enthusiasts, and anglers flock to the many lakes impounded on the Verde and Salt Rivers northeast of the valley.

The valley is home to far too many events, museums, and other cultural activities to mention them all, but here are a few highlights. The Arizona Science Center offers hands-on science exhibits that appeal to kids. Adults should check out the Arizona Museum of History. If you're an art lover, don't miss the Phoenix Art Museum; for Native American arts and crafts, visit the Heard Museum. Children ages 4 to 12 will enjoy a wonderful hands-on art experience at the Arizona Museum for Youth in Mesa. If you're into airplanes, the Champlin Fighter Museum, also in Mesa, has a fine collection of authentic planes from World Wars I and II.

In Coolidge, check out Casa Grande Ruins National Monument, which preserves a striking example of prehistoric Hohokam Indian architecture. The Hohokam people lived in the Valley of the Sun for hundreds of years and built a thriving community based on farming by diverting the water of the Salt River through a valley-wide system of canals. In Phoenix, Pueblo Grande Museum and Cultural Park exhibits some of the Hohokam artifacts. Another place to learn about the valley's history is the Pioneer Living History Museum north of Phoenix. The Desert Botanical Garden is a great place to learn more about desert natural history.

For more information:

Phoenix and Valley of the Sun Convention and Visitors Bureau

400 E. Van Buren, Ste. 600

Phoenix, AZ 85004

(602) 254-6500; (800) CALLPHX

www.visitphoenix.com

Canyon Lake near Tortilla Flats Campground

Number	Name	Elevation	Season	RV/Trailer	Sites	Water	RV dump	Fishing	Hiking trails	Boating	Boat launch	Wheelchair access	Fee	Stay limit, days
63	Estrella Mountain Regional Park	1,000	Year-round	•	7	•	•		•				•	14
64	White Tank Mountains Regional Park	1,400	Year-round	•	40	•	•		•				•	14
65	Lake Pleasant Regional Park	1,800	Year-round	•	148	•	•	•	•	•	•	•	•	14
66	Cave Creek Recreation Area	1,900	Year-round	•	38	•	•	•	•	•	•		•	14
67	Horseshoe	1,900	Year-round	•	12			•		•	•			14
68	Riverside	1,600	Year-round	•	12	•		•		•				14
69	Mesquite	1,900	Year-round	•	12	•		•		•			•	14
70	McDowell Mountain Regional Park	2,000	Year-round	•	76	•	•	•	•			•	•	14
71	Usery Mountain Regional Park	2,000	Year-round	•	73	•	•	•	•			•	•	14
72	Lost Dutchman State Park	1,800	Year-round	•	35	•			•			•	•	14
73	Tortilla	1,800	Oct–Apr	•	77	•			•			•	•	14

63 Estrella Mountain Regional Park

Location: About 23 miles southwest of Phoenix, in the foothills of the Estrella Mountains
Sites: 7 RV with no size limit; full hookups
Road conditions: Paved
Management: Maricopa County Parks and Recreation Department, (623) 932-3811, www.maricopa.gov/parks/estrella
Finding the campground: From downtown Phoenix, go about 16 miles west on I-10; turn left at exit 126 onto Estrella Parkway. Follow the signs 7 miles to the park and campground.
About the campground: The park and campground are located at the north end of the rugged Sierra Estrella. There are 35 miles of trails, as well as a golf course and a rodeo arena. Group camping is available. Seven sites with water and electrical hookups.Some partial hookups are available, as are showers. The nearest full services are in Phoenix.

64 White Tank Mountains Regional Park

Location: About 33 miles west of Phoenix, in the foothills of the White Tank Mountains
Sites: 40 tent and RV with no size limit; no hookups
Road conditions: Paved
Management: Maricopa County Parks and Recreation Department, (623) 935-2505, www.maricopa.gov/parks/white_tank

Finding the campground: From Phoenix, go about 18 miles west on I-10. Exit at Cotton Lane, then go north 7 miles. Turn left onto Olive Avenue and continue about 8 miles, past the park entrance, to the campground near the end of White Tanks Mountain Drive.

About the campground: The park and campground are located in the eastern foothills of the White Tank Mountains, in the Sonoran Desert. There are 29 miles of trails for hikers, equestrians, and mountain bikers. A group camp area and a playground are available, as are showers. The nearest services are in Phoenix.

65 Lake Pleasant Regional Park

Location: About 36 miles northwest of Phoenix, off AZ 74 at Lake Pleasant
Sites: 148 RV with no size limit; some full hookups
Road conditions: Paved
Management: Maricopa County Parks and Recreation Department, (928) 501-1710, www.maricopa.gov/parks/lake_pleasant
Finding the campground: From downtown Phoenix, go about 24 miles north on I-17; exit at Carefree Highway. Go left (west) 5 miles, and turn right (north) onto AZ 74; drive 6 miles to the park entrance signs.
About the campground: This is a desert campground, so it will be hot in summer. There are 26 sites with water and electrical hookups, and showers are available. Fishing, boating, waterskiing, sailboarding, and other water sports are popular on Lake Pleasant. Boat rentals are available. The campground could be used as a base for exploring the rugged Hieroglyphic Mountains to the northwest. The nearest full services are in Phoenix.

66 Cave Creek Recreation Area

Location: About 33 miles north of Phoenix, in the foothills of the New River Mountains
Sites: 38 RV with no size limit; some full hookups
Road conditions: Paved
Management: Maricopa County Parks and Recreation Department, (623) 465-0431, www.maricopa.gov/parks/cave_creek
Finding the campground: From downtown Phoenix, drive about 24 miles north on I-17; exit at AZ 74 (Carefree Highway). Go 6 miles east to 32nd Street, turn left, and go 3 miles to the recreation area entrance.
About the campground: The recreation area and campground are in the Sonoran Desert foothills near Cave Creek. It features both hiking and horse trails; horse rentals are available. Mountain biking is also popular in the area. Electrical and water hookups are available, as are showers. The nearest services are in Cave Creek; the nearest full services are in Phoenix.

67 Horseshoe

Location: 21 miles northeast of Carefree, on the Verde River
Sites: 12 tent and RV up to 22 feet; no hookups
Road conditions: Paved, dirt
Management: Tonto National Forest, (602) 225-5200, www.fs.usda.gov/main/tonto/home
Finding the campground: From Carefree, go 5 miles east on Cave Creek Road, then turn right onto Bartlett Dam Road (FR 205). After 6 miles, turn left onto Horseshoe Dam Road and continue 10 miles.
About the campground: This Sonoran Desert campground is on the Verde River below Horseshoe Dam. Fishing and boating are popular on the river. The nearest services are in Carefree; the nearest full services are in Phoenix.

68 Riverside

Location: About 23 miles east of Carefree, on the Verde River
Sites: 12 tent
Road conditions: Paved, dirt
Management: Tonto National Forest, (602) 225-5200, www.fs.usda.gov/main/tonto/home
Finding the campground: From Carefree, go 5 miles east on Cave Creek Road, then turn right onto Bartlett Dam Road (FR 205). Drive 16 miles; turn right and go 3 miles to the campground.
About the campground: Located in the Sonoran Desert below Bartlett Dam, this campground is a popular access point on the Verde River. Boating, rafting, and fishing are popular activities on the river. The nearest services are in Carefree; the nearest full services are in Phoenix.

The Sonoran Desert in central and southern Arizona has two rainy seasons, which makes it the lushest of the four American deserts.

69 Mesquite

Location: About 23 miles east of Carefree, on the Verde River
Sites: 12 tent and RV up to 16 feet
Road conditions: Paved, dirt
Management: Tonto National Forest, (602) 225-5200, www.fs.usda.gov/main/tonto/home
Finding the campground: From Carefree, go 5 miles east on Cave Creek Road, then turn right onto Bartlett Dam Road (FR 205). Drive 6 miles to the junction of FR 19 and FR 205. Turn left to stay on FR 205, and drive 9 miles north to the campground.
About the campground: Located on the Verde River below Horseshoe Dam, this Sonoran Desert campground is a popular river access point. There are no hookups. Boating, rafting, and fishing are popular activities on the river. The nearest services are in Carefree; the nearest full services are in Phoenix.

70 McDowell Mountain Regional Park

Location: About 22 miles east of Scottsdale
Sites: 76 tent and RV; water and electric hookups
Road conditions: Paved
Management: Maricopa County Parks and Recreation Department, (480) 471-0173, www.maricopa.gov/parks/mcdowell
Finding the campground: From Scottsdale, go east on Shea Boulevard, then turn left onto Fountain Hills Boulevard, which becomes McDowell Mountain Road. Turn left at the park entrance, and follow the signs to the family campground.
About the campground: The park, located in the northeast foothills of the McDowell Mountains, features hiking, riding, and mountain bike trails. Group camping is available by reservation. Limited services are available in Fountain Hills; there are full services in Phoenix.

71 Usery Mountain Regional Park

Location: About 12 miles northeast of Mesa
Sites: 73 tent and RV; water and electrical hookups
Road conditions: Paved
Management: Maricopa County Parks and Recreation Department, (480) 984-0032, www.maricopa.gov/parks/usery
Finding the campground: From Mesa, drive about 12 miles north on Ellsworth Road, which becomes Usery Pass Road. Turn right onto the park entrance road, and follow the signs to the family campground.
About the campground: The desert campground is located in the Usery Mountains and features an extensive system of hiking, riding, and mountain biking trails. Group camping is available by reservation. Full services are available in Mesa.

72 Lost Dutchman State Park

Location: About 5 miles northeast of Apache Junction, in the foothills of the Superstition Mountains
Sites: 35 tent and RV; electrical and water hookups
Road conditions: Paved
Management: Lost Dutchman State Park, (480) 982-4455, azstateparks.com/Parks/LODU
Finding the campground: From Apache Junction, go north 5 miles on AZ 88.
About the campground: The park's dramatic setting in the Sonoran Desert at the base of the Superstition Mountains is a good jumping-off point for exploration of the area. The park features nature trails, and the nearby Superstition Wilderness has many miles of backcountry trails. Full services are available in Apache Junction.

73 Tortilla

Location: About 18 miles northeast of Apache Junction, in the Superstition Mountains
Sites: 77 tent and RV up to 22 feet; no hookups
Road conditions: Paved
Management: Tonto National Forest, (602) 225-5200, www.fs.usda.gov/main/tonto/home
Finding the campground: From Apache Junction, go 18 miles northeast on AZ 88, past Canyon Lake.
About the campground: Surrounded by the famous Superstition Mountains, this campground makes a good base to explore the historic Apache Trail (AZ 88) and the surrounding area. The Superstition Wilderness, to the south, features a network of backcountry trails. A post office, restaurant, and gift shop are located at Tortilla Flat Resort across the road from the campground. It's 2 miles west to Canyon Lake, which has cold- and warm-water fisheries and a full-service marina with boat rentals, a restaurant, and lake tours. The nearest full services are in Apache Junction.

High Country

Arizona's High Country is a camping and outdoor recreation paradise. It's somewhat misnamed, because it includes nearly 2 vertical miles of elevation, ranging from 2,000 feet in the Sonoran Desert country in the Tonto Basin to 11,403-foot Mount Baldy in the White Mountains. The High Country contains the ruggedly beautiful country south of the Mogollon Rim around Payson, includes the central Mogollon Rim around Show Low, and encompasses the fir and spruce forests of the White Mountains around Alpine. Three national forests, the Tonto, the Apache, and the Sitgreaves, are responsible for managing most of the area. The White Mountain and San Carlos Apache Tribes manage much of the land south of the central Mogollon Rim. Dozens of mountain lakes provide diverse fishing, boating, paddling, and other water sports. Spectacular Salt River Canyon is one of the premier whitewater rivers in the state.

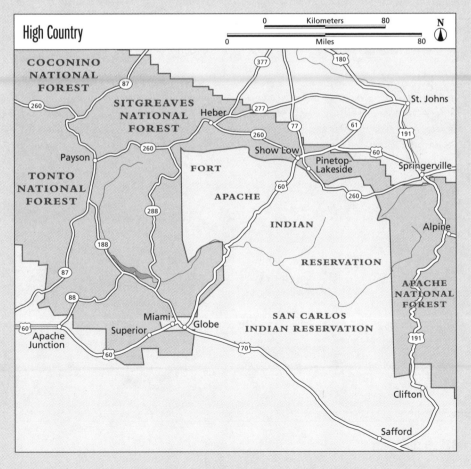

Payson

Payson is in the center of the mountain country made famous by western writer Zane Grey, who often wrote from a small cabin close beneath the 2,000-foot escarpment of the Mogollon Rim. Just a ninety-minute drive from Phoenix, the Payson area is a popular summer retreat. The Mazatzal Wilderness, one of the largest in the state, bounds the area on the west. Containing the northern half of the Mazatzal Mountains, this craggy range has miles of trails for the backcountry hiker. The smaller Hellsgate Wilderness contains Tonto and Haigler Creeks, which form deep, rugged canyons. Miles of forest roads and trails are open to mountain bikers. Probably the best-known trail is the Highline National Recreation Trail, which winds under the Mogollon Rim for miles. And, yes, there are campgrounds! In addition to the standard USDA Forest Service campgrounds listed here, the Tonto National Forest has a number of small, primitive campsites scattered through the forest. You can camp dispersed nearly anywhere in the forest.

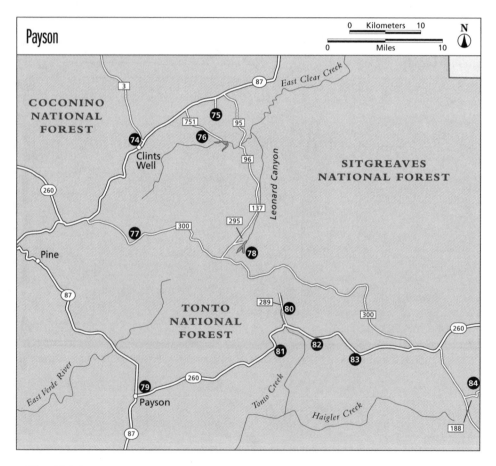

In Payson, check out the Zane Grey and Rim Country Museums to learn more about the history of the region. North of Payson you can visit the world's largest travertine natural bridge at Tonto Natural Bridge State Park. Visit the Tonto Creek Fish Hatchery to see how trout and other fish are raised and stocked.

For more information:

Rim Country Regional Chamber of Commerce
100 W. Main St.
PO Box 1380
Payson, AZ 85547
(928) 474-4515; (800) 672-9766
www.rimcountrychamber.com

Buck Springs Cabin is one of several historic sites to explore on the Mogollon Rim.

Number	Name	Elevation	Season	RV/Trailer	Sites	Water	RV dump	Fishing	Hiking trails	Boating	Boat launch	Wheelchair access	Fee	Stay limit, days
74	Clints Well	7,000	Year-round	•	7									14
75	Blue Ridge	7,300	Apr-Sept	•	10	•			•				•	14
76	Rock Crossing	7,500	Apr-Sept	•	34	•		•	•	•	•		•	14
77	Kehl Springs	7,500	Year-round	•	8									14
78	Knoll Lake	7,400	May-Sept	•	33	•		•	•	•	•		•	14
79	Houston Mesa	5,100	Year-round	•	75	•	•	•	•				•	14
80	Upper Tonto Creek	5,600	Apr-Oct	•	9	•	•	•					•	14
81	Ponderosa	5,600	Apr-Oct	•	61	•	•	•	•				•	14
82	Christopher Creek	5,800	Apr-Oct	•	43	•	•	•				•	•	14
83	Sharp Creek	6,000	Apr-Oct	•	28	•	•					•	•	14
84	Valentine Ridge	6,700	May-Oct	•	9									14

74 Clints Well

Location: About 52 miles southeast of Flagstaff, on the Mogollon Plateau
Sites: 7 tent and RV up to 22 feet; no hookups
Road conditions: Paved
Management: Coconino National Forest, (928) 527-3620, www.fs.usda.gov/main/coconino/home
Finding the campground: From Flagstaff, drive 51 miles south on Lake Mary Road, CR 3. The campground is on the right, just before the junction with AZ 87.
About the campground: Located in tall, old-growth ponderosa pines, Clints Well Campground is a convenient base for exploring the Mogollon Rim country, easily accessible from numerous forest roads leading off CR 3 and AZ 87. Unlimited mountain biking is possible on the forest roads, many of which are winding, unimproved tracks. There are several hiking areas in the vicinity, including the historic Cabin Loop trail system, the Arizona Trail, and the West Clear Creek Wilderness. Trails also lead into East Clear Creek. Limited services are available at Clints Well; the nearest full services are in Payson and Winslow.

75 Blue Ridge

Location: About 60 miles southeast of Flagstaff, on the Mogollon Plateau
Sites: 10 tent and RV up to 22 feet; no hookups
Road conditions: All-weather dirt
Management: Coconino National Forest, (928) 527-3620, www.fs.usda.gov/main/coconino/home

Finding the campground: From Flagstaff, drive 51 miles south on Lake Mary Road, CR 3, then turn left on AZ 87. Continue 8 miles; turn right onto FR 138 and go 1 mile.

About the campground: This small campground is located in a stately pine forest. It's a good base for exploring the Mogollon Plateau and its canyons and streams. The 800-mile Arizona Trail passes through this campground on its way from Utah to Mexico, and there are other hiking trails in the area. Miles of two-track forest roads provide good mountain biking. Fishing and boating are popular on Blue Ridge Reservoir, a small lake in a deep canyon. Limited services are available in Clints Well; the nearest full services are in Winslow.

76 Rock Crossing

Location: About 59 miles southeast of Flagstaff, near Blue Ridge Reservoir
Sites: 34 tent and RV up to 22 feet; no hookups
Road conditions: All-weather dirt
Management: Coconino National Forest, (928) 527-3620, www.fs.usda.gov/main/coconino/home
Finding the campground: From Flagstaff, drive 51 miles south on Lake Mary Road, CR 3, then turn left on AZ 87. Continue 5 miles; turn right onto FR 751 and go 3 miles to the campground on the right.
About the campground: Located in the pine forest near Blue Ridge Reservoir, the campground is named for a nearby crossing of East Clear Creek. Many canyons cut through the Mogollon Plateau, and crossing points are limited. Rock Crossing is usually submerged under Blue Ridge Reservoir,

Blue Ridge Reservoir near Rock Crossing Campground

but other historic crossings are still in use. The reservoir is 3 miles away and is a popular fishing lake. It's also a good lake for paddlers—the narrow canyons are the next best thing to a river trip. Limited services are available in Clints Well; the nearest full services are in Winslow and Payson.

77 Kehl Springs

Location: About 66 miles southeast of Flagstaff, on the Mogollon Rim
Sites: 8 tent and RV up to 22 feet; no hookups
Road conditions: Dirt
Management: Coconino National Forest, (928) 527-3620, www.fs.usda.gov/main/coconino/home
Finding the campground: From Flagstaff, drive 51 miles south on Lake Mary Road, CR 3, then turn right onto AZ 87. Continue 9 miles, and turn left onto FR 300 (this turnoff is 27 miles north of Payson). Go 6 miles to the campground.
About the campground: This small campground is near the edge of the Mogollon Rim in a stand of shady ponderosa pines. It's also right on the Rim Road, a scenic drive along the top of the Mogollon Rim, and near the historic Crook Trail. During the Apache Wars, General Crook built a military wagon road along the rim to connect a number of US Army forts. The approximate route of the wagon road is followed by FR 300; the exact route has been marked by the USDA Forest Service. Hiking and mountain biking are virtually unlimited on the many trails and roads on the plateau north of the rim. Limited services are available at Clints Well; the nearest full services are in Payson.

78 Knoll Lake

Location: About 90 miles southeast of Flagstaff, on the Mogollon Rim
Sites: 33 tent and RV up to 22 feet; no hookups
Road conditions: Dirt
Management: Coconino National Forest, (928) 527-3620, www.fs.usda.gov/main/coconino/home
Finding the campground: From Flagstaff, drive 51 miles south on Lake Mary Road, CR 3, then turn right onto AZ 87. Continue 9 miles, and turn left onto FR 300 (this turnoff is 27 miles north of Payson). Go 23 miles, and turn left onto FR 295E and go 4 miles to the campground.
About the campground: The campground and lake are several miles north of the Mogollon Rim, in ponderosa pine forest. Fishing and boating are popular on this small but scenic lake. The surrounding rim country offers many opportunities for mountain biking, hiking, and exploring. The nearest full services are in Payson.

79 Houston Mesa

Location: North side of Payson

Sites: 75 tent and RV up to 30 feet; no hookups

Road conditions: Paved

Management: Tonto National Forest, (602) 225-5200, www.fs.usda.gov/main/tonto/home ; reservations (877) 444-6777, www.recreation.gov

Finding the campground: From Payson, drive to the north end of town on AZ 87, and turn left onto FR 199.

About the campground: This campground is conveniently located just north of Payson. A great starting point for exploring the Payson area and the rim country, the campground also has a nature trail. The nearest full services are in Payson.

80 Upper Tonto Creek

Location: About 16 miles northeast of Payson, on Tonto Creek

Sites: 9 tent and RV up to 22 feet; no hookups

Road conditions: Paved

Management: Tonto National Forest, (602) 225-5200, www.fs.usda.gov/main/tonto/home

Finding the campground: From Payson, drive 15 miles northeast on AZ 260, and turn left onto FR 289. Continue about 1 mile to the campground.

About the campground: The campground is on Tonto Creek below the Mogollon Rim. There are many hiking trails in the area, including the Highline National Recreation Trail, which runs for more than 25 miles under the ramparts of the Mogollon Rim. Fishing is popular in the creek. Limited services are available at Christopher Creek; the nearest full services are in Payson.

81 Ponderosa

Location: About 12 miles northeast of Payson, below the Mogollon Rim

Sites: 61 tent and RV up to 60 feet; no hookups

Road conditions: Paved

Management: Tonto National Forest, (602) 225-5200, www.fs.usda.gov/main/tonto/home; reservations (877) 444-6777, www.recreation.gov

Finding the campground: From Payson, drive 12 miles northeast on AZ 260; turn right into the campground.

About the campground: The campground features a self-guided nature trail. Additional hikes include trails into the nearby Hellsgate Wilderness and the Highline National Recreation Trail and its side trails. Group camping is available. Some services are available in Christopher Creek; the nearest full services are in Payson.

82 Christopher Creek

Location: About 19 miles northeast of Payson, on Christopher Creek
Sites: 43 tent and RV up to 22 feet; no hookups
Road conditions: Paved
Management: Tonto National Forest, (602) 225-5200, www.fs.usda.gov/main/tonto/home
Finding the campground: From Payson, drive 19 miles northeast on AZ 260; turn right into the campground.
About the campground: Fishing is popular in Christopher Creek, a cold trout stream that issues from springs below the Mogollon Rim. Limited services are available in Christopher Creek; the nearest full services are in Payson.

83 Sharp Creek

Location: About 23 miles east of Payson, near AZ 260
Sites: 28 tent and RV up to 45 feet; no hookups
Road conditions: Dirt
Management: Tonto National Forest, (602) 225-5200, www.fs.usda.gov/main/tonto/home; reservations (877) 444-6777, www.recreation.gov
Finding the campground: From Payson, go 23 miles east on AZ 260; turn right into the campground.
About the campground: This campground is a good base for exploring the rugged country below the Mogollon Rim. The 260 trailhead, 3 miles east on AZ 260, provides access to the east end of the Highline National Recreation Trail. Woods Canyon and Willow Springs Lakes are located off AZ 260 on the Mogollon Rim. Limited services are available in Christopher Creek; there are full services in Payson.

84 Valentine Ridge

Location: About 41 miles east of Payson, below the Mogollon Rim
Sites: 9 tent and RV up to 16 feet; no hookups
Road conditions: Dirt
Management: Tonto National Forest, (602) 225-5200, www.fs.usda.gov/main/tonto/home
Finding the campground: From Payson, go 33 miles east on AZ 260, and turn right onto FR 512. Continue 6 miles; turn left onto FR 188 and go 2 miles to the campground.
About the campground: This is a small campground in an isolated setting below the Mogollon Rim. It's a good base for exploring the central Mogollon Rim country and the Sierra Ancha to the south. A 4-mile mountain bike trail starts in the campground. Limited services are available in Christopher Creek; there are full services in Payson.

Globe

North and west of the small city of Globe is an incredible variety of country, ranging from Sonoran Desert to pine-forested mountains. The Four Peaks, Superstition, Sierra Ancha, Salome, and Salt River Canyon Wildernesses provide backcountry opportunities for hikers and river runners. Miles of forest roads and trails outside the wildernesses offer some great mountain biking. Several large lakes on the Salt River are very popular with boaters and anglers. The largest of these, Theodore Roosevelt Lake, was the first federal reclamation project in the West. The original masonry dam was built from local stone quarried at the site.

Tonto National Monument, near Theodore Roosevelt Lake, preserves a fine example of a cliff dwelling from the Salado people, who occupied the area during the thirteenth through fifteenth centuries. The monument was proclaimed by Theodore Roosevelt, who used the new presidential authority granted by the American Antiquities Act of 1906 to create the nation's first national monuments and national wildlife refuges, starting a presidential tradition that continues to this day. Just outside the town of Superior, you'll find Boyce Thompson Arboretum, a popular birding destination with a variety of habitats. The wildflower displays are exquisite here, and the arboretum provides a special picnic area.

Camping on Theodore Roosevelt Lake

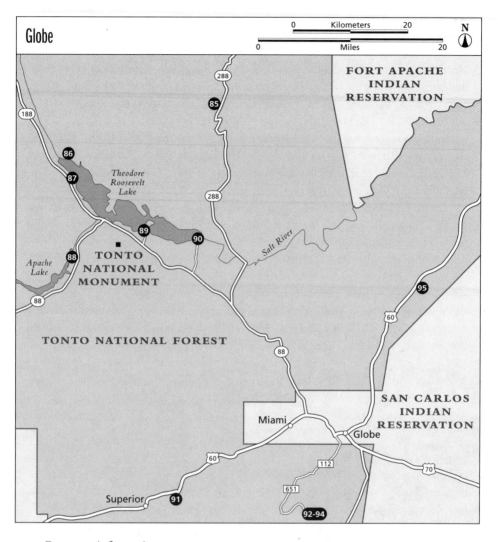

Globe

0 Kilometers 20
0 Miles 20
N

288
85
188
86
87
Theodore
Roosevelt
Lake
288
89
90
Salt River
88
Apache
Lake
TONTO
NATIONAL
MONUMENT
88
95
60

TONTO NATIONAL FOREST

88

FORT APACHE
INDIAN
RESERVATION

SAN CARLOS
INDIAN
RESERVATION

Miami
Globe

60
112
70
651

Superior
91
92-94

For more information:
Globe-Miami Chamber of Commerce
1360 N. Broad St.
Globe, AZ 85501
(928) 425-4495; (800) 804-5623
www.globemiamichamber.com

Superior Chamber of Commerce
PO Box 95
Superior, AZ 85173
(520) 689-0200
www.superiorazchamber.net

Number	Name	Elevation	Season	RV/Trailer	Sites	Water	RV dump	Fishing	Hiking trails	Boating	Boat launch	Wheelchair access	Fee	Stay limit, days
85	Rose Creek	5,400	May–Oct	•	5									14
86	Indian Point	2,200	Year-round	•	54	•		•	•	•	•	•	•	14
87	Cholla	2,200	Year-round	•	206	•	•	•	•	•	•	•	•	14
88	Burnt Corral	1,900	Year-round	•	82	•		•			•		•	14
89	Windy Hill	2,200	Year-round	•	347	•	•	•	•	•	•	•	•	14
90	Schoolhouse	2,200	Year-round	•	211	•		•			•	•	•	14
91	Oak Flat	4,200	Year-round	•	16				•					14
92	Pinal	7,500	May–Nov	•	16				•					14
93	Pioneer Pass	6,000	May–Nov	•	23				•					14
94	Sulphide del Rey	4,500	Year-round	•	10									14
95	Jones Water	4,500	Year-round	•	12									14

85 Rose Creek

Location: About 41 miles north of Globe, in the Sierra Ancha
Sites: 5 tent and RV up to 16 feet; no hookups
Road conditions: Paved, all-weather dirt
Management: Tonto National Forest, (602) 225-5200, www.fs.usda.gov/main/tonto/home
Finding the campground: From Globe, go about 4 miles west on US 60 and turn right onto AZ 88. Continue 13 miles, and then turn right onto AZ 288. Continue 24 miles; turn left onto FR 152 and go 0.25 mile to the campground.
About the campground: This small, remote campground is a fine base for exploring the nearby Sierra Ancha and Salome Wildernesses, which have a number of hiking trails. The nearest services are in Young; the nearest full services are in Globe.

86 Indian Point

Location: About 46 miles northwest of Globe, on Theodore Roosevelt Lake
Sites: 54 tent and RV up to 16 feet; no hookups
Road conditions: Paved, dirt
Management: Tonto National Forest, (602) 225-5200, www.fs.usda.gov/main/tonto/home
Finding the campground: From Globe, drive about 4 miles west on US 60 and turn right onto AZ 88. Continue 28 miles to Roosevelt Dam; turn right and continue 10 miles on AZ 188. Turn right onto FR 60 and go 2 miles; turn right onto FR 661 and continue 2 miles to the campground.

About the campground: This campground is on the northwest end of Roosevelt Lake. It's a low-elevation desert campground, popular with anglers, boaters, and water sports enthusiasts during the fall, winter, and spring. The nearest services are in Roosevelt; the nearest full services are in Globe.

87 Cholla

Location: About 38 miles northwest of Globe, on Theodore Roosevelt Lake
Sites: 206 tent and RV up to 32 feet; no hookups
Road conditions: Paved
Management: Tonto National Forest, (602) 225-5200, www.fs.usda.gov/main/tonto/home
Finding the campground: From Globe, drive about 4 miles west on US 60 and turn right onto AZ 88. Continue 28 miles to Roosevelt Dam and continue across Roosevelt Lake Bridge on AZ 188. Go 6 miles to the campground, which is on the right.
About the campground: This desert campground on the shore of Roosevelt Lake is the largest completely solar-operated campground in the country. Open year-round, it is hot in summer. A public boat launch provides ready access to the huge reservoir for anglers, boaters, and water sports enthusiasts. Nearby Tonto National Monument preserves a fine set of Native American ruins, and the Superstition Wilderness to the south has an extensive network of backcountry trails. The nearest services are in Roosevelt; the nearest full services are in Globe.

88 Burnt Corral

Location: About 38 miles northwest of Globe, on Apache Lake
Sites: 82 tent and RV up to 22 feet; no hookups
Road conditions: Paved, all-weather dirt
Management: Tonto National Forest, (602) 225-5200, www.fs.usda.gov/main/tonto/home
Finding the campground: From Globe, drive about 4 miles west on US 60 and turn right onto AZ 88. Continue 28 miles to Roosevelt Dam; turn left and continue 6 miles. Turn right onto FR 183 and go less than a mile to the campground.
About the campground: Located right on the shore of Apache Lake, this low-elevation desert campground has a boat launch and is popular with anglers, boaters, and water sports enthusiasts. The nearest services are in Roosevelt; the nearest full services are in Globe.

89 Windy Hill

Location: About 30 miles northwest of Globe, on Theodore Roosevelt Lake

Sites: 347 tent and RV up to 32 feet; no hookups

Road conditions: Paved, dirt

Management: Tonto National Forest, (602) 225-5200, www.fs.usda.gov/main/tonto/home

Finding the campground: From Globe, drive about 4 miles west on US 60, and turn right onto AZ 88. Continue 25 miles to FR 82; turn right and go about 1.5 miles to the campground.

About the campground: Another desert campground on the shore of Roosevelt Lake, this is the largest USDA Forest Service campground in the country. Though it is open year-round, it is hot in summer. There is a public boat launch. The campground is also a possible base for exploring the nearby Superstition Wilderness. The nearest services are in Roosevelt; the nearest full services are in Globe.

Four Peaks towers above Tonto Basin

90 Schoolhouse

Location: About 20 miles west of Globe, on the east end of Theodore Roosevelt Lake
Sites: 211 tent and RV; no hookups
Road conditions: Paved, dirt
Management: Tonto National Forest, (602) 225-5200, www.fs.usda.gov/main/tonto/home
Finding the campground: From Globe, drive about 4 miles west on US 60, and turn right onto AZ 88. Continue 20 miles to FR 447, turn right, and go 4 miles to the campground.
About the campground: This desert campground is on the eastern shore of Roosevelt Lake. Normally open year-round, the campground closes when Roosevelt Lake drops below 2,110 feet. There is a public boat launch. The campground is also a river access point for the Salt River, which enters the lake from the east. The nearest services are in Roosevelt; the nearest full services are in Globe.

91 Oak Flat

Location: About 18 miles southwest of Globe
Sites: 16 tent and RV up to 22 feet; no hookups
Road conditions: Paved
Management: Tonto National Forest, (602) 225-5200, www.fs.usda.gov/main/tonto/home
Finding the campground: From Globe, drive about 18 miles west on US 60, then right onto FR 469, and then turn left into the campground. (This turnoff is about 4 miles east of Superior.)
About the campground: This campground is pleasant year-round because of its moderate elevation in an oak and piñon pine–juniper flat. Its main attraction is its convenient location for the traveler. Devils Canyon and Apache Leap are nearby attractions for the backcountry explorer. Limited services are in Superior; full services are available in Globe.

92 Pinal

Location: 15 miles south of Globe, in the Pinal Mountains
Sites: 16 tent and RV up to 16 feet; no hookups
Road conditions: Paved, dirt
Management: Tonto National Forest, (602) 225-5200, www.fs.usda.gov/main/tonto/home
Finding the campground: From Globe, drive south on Jess Hayes Road to the junction of FR 112 and FR 222. Continue on FR 112 for 2.5 miles; turn right onto FR 55 and go 2.5 miles. At the junction of FR 55 and FR 651, turn left and drive 9.0 miles to the campground.
About the campground: This pair of small campgrounds is located high on the pine- and fir-forested slopes of Pinal Mountain, a popular cool mountain escape in the Globe area. A network of forest roads offers mountain bikers a chance to explore. Full services are available in Globe.

93 Pioneer Pass

Location: 9 miles south of Globe, in the Pinal Mountains
Sites: 23 tent and RV up to 16 feet; no hookups
Road conditions: Paved, dirt
Management: Tonto National Forest, (602) 225-5200, www.fs.usda.gov/main/tonto/home
Finding the campground: From Globe, drive south on Jess Hayes Road to the junction of FR 112 and FR 222. Continue on FR 112 for 9 miles to the campground.
About the campground: This campground is located high on the pine- and fir-forested slopes of Pinal Mountain, a popular mountain escape in the Globe area. A network of forest roads offers mountain bikers a chance to explore the scenic mountains. Full services are available in Globe.

94 Sulphide del Rey

Location: 10 miles south of Globe, in the Pinal Mountains
Sites: 10 tent and RV under 20 feet, no hookups
Road conditions: Paved, dirt
Management: Tonto National Forest, (602) 225-5200, www.fs.usda.gov/main/tonto/home
Finding the campground: From Globe, drive south on Jess Hayes Road to the junction of FR 112 and FR 222. Continue on FR 112 for 2.5 miles; turn right onto FR 55 and go 2.5 miles. At the junction of FR 55 and FR 651, turn left and drive 5.0 miles to the campground.
About the campground: Set in a fine stand of ponderosa pine, this area was the site of an old mining community. The miners lived here to escape of the heat of the lower elevations, where the mine was located. Full services are available in Globe.

95 Jones Water

Location: 18 miles northeast of Globe
Sites: 12 tent and RV up to 16 feet; no hookups
Road conditions: Paved
Management: Tonto National Forest, (602) 225-5200, www.fs.usda.gov/main/tonto/home
Finding the campground: From Globe, drive 18 miles northeast on US 60; the campground is on the right.
About the campground: The main attraction of this small campground is its convenient location right along the highway, although the surrounding country would be interesting to explore. The nearest services are in Globe.

Show Low

Show Low and its close neighbor, Pinetop-Lakeside, are located at the eastern end of the central Mogollon Rim in Apache-Sitgreaves National Forest. Both towns have become very popular summer retreats for the desert dwellers of Phoenix and Tucson. The small town of Heber is near the western end. Stretching for miles, the Mogollon Plateau country, just north of the rim itself, is a pine-forested plateau cut by numerous canyons that drain northward. Dozens of small, man-made lakes dot these canyons and provide both angling and boating. Many of the lakes are limited to small gas or electric motors, so they are enjoyable for canoeists and other paddlers. Many of the campgrounds in the area are located at or near the lakes. Mountain bikers can enjoy great cruises on miles of cool, shady forest roads.

North of Show Low you can get an idea of what it was like to settle this country by touring some of the one hundred pioneer homes preserved in the town of Snowflake. Visit Fort Apache Historic Park near Whiteriver for a perspective on the history of Apache country. Fort Apache was an important post for the army troops led by General George Crook during the Apache wars of the nineteenth century. The Apache Cultural Center preserves the rich heritage of the Apache people.

Boating is popular on Woods Canyon Lake and several other lakes along the central Mogollon Rim.

Show Low

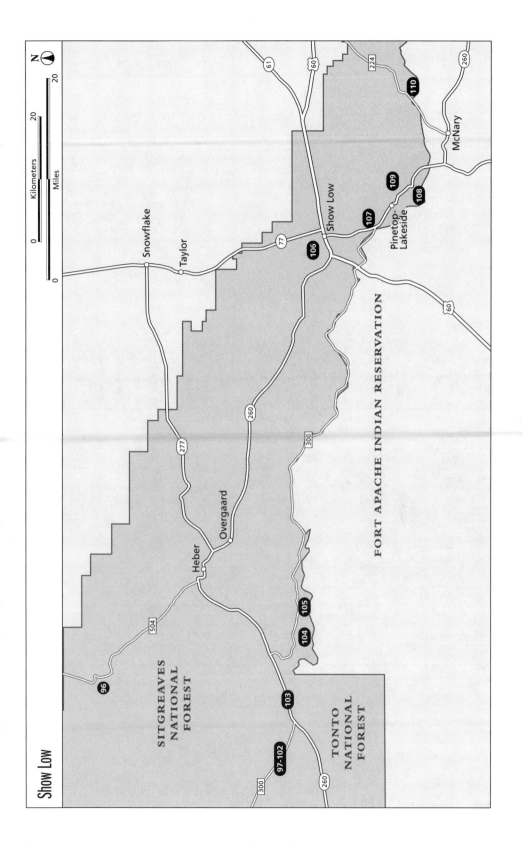

For more information:
Pinetop–Lakeside Chamber of Commerce
102-C W. White Mountain Blvd.
Lakeside, AZ 85935
(928) 367-4290; (800) 573-4031
www.pinetoplakesidechamber.com

Show Low Chamber of Commerce
81 E. Deuce of Clubs
Show Low, AZ 85901
(928) 537-2326
www.showlowchamber.com

Snowflake-Taylor Chamber of Commerce
www.snowflaketaylorchamber.com

Number	Name	Elevation	Season	RV/Trailer	Sites	Water	RV dump	Fishing	Hiking trails	Boating	Boat launch	Wheelchair access	Fee	Stay limit, days
96	Chevelon Crossing	6,500	Mar–Dec.	•	7				•					14
97	Spillway	7,500	May–Sep.	•	26	•		•	•	•	•	•	•	14
98	Crook	7,500	May–Oct	•	26	•	•	•	•				•	14
99	Aspen	7,500	May–Oct	•	136	•		•	•	•	•	•	•	14
100	Mogollon	7,500	May–Oct	•	26	•		•	•	•		•	•	14
101	Rim	7,500	May–Sep.	•	26	•		•	•	•		•		14
102	Sinkhole	7,500	May–Oct	•	26	•		•	•	•	•	•		14
103	Canyon Point	7,600	May–Oct	•	106	•	•	•	•	•	•	•	•	14
104	Black Canyon Rim	7,600	May–Nov.	•	21	•		•		•		•		14
105	Gentry	7,700	May–Nov.		5									14
106	Fool Hollow Lake Recreation Area	6,300	Year-round	•	123	•	•	•		•	•	•	•	14
107	Show Low Lake	7,000	Year-round	•	75	•	•	•		•	•	•	•	14
108	Lakeside	7,000	May–Sep.	•	83	•						•	•	14
109	Scott Reservoir	6,740	Year-round		12		•			•	•			14
110	Los Burros	7,900	May–Oct	•	10				•					14

Chevelon Lake

96 Chevelon Crossing

Location: About 19 miles northwest of Heber, in Chevelon Canyon

Sites: 7 tent and RV up to 16 feet; no hookups

Road conditions: Paved, all-weather dirt

Management: Apache-Sitgreaves National Forest, (928) 333-4301, www.fs.usda.gov/asnf

Finding the campground: From Heber, drive 1 mile west on AZ 260 and turn right onto FR 504. Continue 18 miles to the campground.

About the campground: This small, remote campground is a good choice if you want to get away from the crowds. It's also a good base for exploring Chevelon Canyon with its permanent stream and the Mogollon Plateau country. Limited services are available in Heber; the nearest full services are in Winslow.

97 Spillway

Location: About 26 miles west of Heber, near Woods Canyon Lake
Sites: 26 tent and RV up to 16 feet; no hookups
Road conditions: Paved
Management: Apache-Sitgreaves National Forest, (928) 333-4301, www.fs.usda.gov/asnf; reservations (877) 444-6777, www.recreation.gov
Finding the campground: From Heber, drive 22 miles west on AZ 260 and turn right onto FR 300. Go 3 miles and turn right onto FR 105. Bear right to reach the campground in about 1 mile.
About the campground: One of several campgrounds in the pines near Woods Canyon Lake, this campground is popular with anglers. It's also near the Mogollon Rim and the historic General Crook Trail, so it makes a good base for exploring the rim country. Easy accessibility from the highway means the campground will fill up early on summer weekends. A group campground is also available. Limited supplies are available nearby. The nearest full services are in Heber.

98 Crook

Location: About 25 miles west of Heber, near Woods Canyon Lake
Sites: 26 tent and RV up to 16 feet; no hookups
Road conditions: Paved
Management: Apache-Sitgreaves National Forest, (928) 333-4301, www.fs.usda.gov/asnf; reservations (877) 444-6777, www.recreation.gov
Finding the campground: From Heber, drive 22 miles west on AZ 260 and turn right onto FR 300. Go 3 miles and turn right onto FR 105.
About the campground: Another campground in the pines near Woods Canyon Lake, this campground is popular with anglers. Easy accessibility from the highway means the campground fills up early on summer weekends. The nearest full services are in Heber.

99 Aspen

Location: About 25 miles west of Heber, near Woods Canyon Lake
Sites: 136 tent and RV up to 32 feet; no hookups
Road conditions: Paved
Management: Apache-Sitgreaves National Forest, (928) 333-4301, www.fs.usda.gov/asnf; reservations (877) 444-6777, www.recreation.gov
Finding the campground: From Heber, drive 22 miles west on AZ 260 and turn right onto FR 300. Go 3 miles and turn right onto FR 105.
About the campground: This is the largest campground near Woods Canyon Lake. Easy accessibility from the highway means the campground fills up early on summer weekends. It also makes a great base for exploring the rim country by mountain bike, vehicle, or on foot. The nearest full services are in Heber.

100 Mogollon

Location: About 26 miles west of Heber, near Woods Canyon Lake
Sites: 26 tent and RV up to 32 feet; no hookups
Road conditions: Paved
Management: Apache-Sitgreaves National Forest, (928) 333-4301, www.fs.usda.gov/asnf
Finding the campground: From Heber, drive 22 miles west on AZ 260 and turn right onto FR 300. Go 4 miles to the campground, which is on the left.
About the campground: Another campground in the pines near Woods Canyon Lake, this campground is popular with anglers and boaters. Easy accessibility from the highway means the campground fills up early on summer weekends. The nearest full services are in Heber.

101 Rim

Location: About 23 miles west of Heber, near Willow Springs Lake
Sites: 26 tent and RV up to 32 feet; no hookups
Road conditions: Paved
Management: Apache-Sitgreaves National Forest, (928) 333-4301, www.fs.usda.gov/asnf
Finding the campground: From Heber, drive 22 miles west on AZ 260 and turn right onto FR 300. Go less than a mile to the campground, which is on the left.
About the campground: This campground is near Willow Springs Lake, so it's popular with anglers and boaters. It's also near the Mogollon Rim and several historic trails, including the General Crook Historic Trail. The nearest full services are in Heber.

102 Sinkhole

Location: About 21 miles southwest of Heber, near Willow Springs Lake
Sites: 26 tent and RV up to 32 feet; no hookups
Road conditions: Paved
Management: Apache-Sitgreaves National Forest, (928) 333-4301, www.fs.usda.gov/asnf
Finding the campground: From Heber, drive 21 miles west on AZ 260 and turn right onto FR 149.
About the campground: This campground is near Willow Springs Lake, so it's popular with anglers and boaters. It's also near the Mogollon Rim and several historic trails. The nearest full services are in Heber.

Mogollon Rim near Canyon Point Campground

103 Canyon Point

Location: About 18 miles southwest of Heber, near the Mogollon Rim
Sites: 106 tent and RV up to 32 feet; 32 with electric hookups
Road conditions: Paved
Management: Apache-Sitgreaves National Forest, (928) 333-4301, www.fs.usda.gov/asnf; reservations (877) 444-6777, www.recreation.gov
Finding the campground: From Heber, drive 18 miles west on AZ 260 and turn left into the campground.
About the campground: This large campground is near the highway and makes a convenient base for exploring the Mogollon Rim country and the numerous canyons and historic trails in the area. A group campsite is available, as are showers. The nearest full services are in Heber.

104 Black Canyon Rim

Location: About 15 miles southwest of Heber, near the Mogollon Rim
Sites: 21 tent and RV up to 16 feet; no hookups
Road conditions: Paved, dirt
Management: Apache-Sitgreaves National Forest, (928) 333-4301, www.fs.usda.gov/asnf
Finding the campground: From Heber, drive 12 miles west on AZ 260 and turn left onto FR 300. Continue 3 miles to the campground.

About the campground: Located on the historic General Crook Trail not far from the Mogollon Rim, the campground is a good base for exploring the rim country. A network of forest roads provides plenty of riding for mountain bikers. The nearest full services are in Heber.

105 Gentry

Location: About 16 miles southwest of Heber, near the Mogollon Rim
Sites: 5 tent
Road conditions: Paved, dirt
Management: Apache-Sitgreaves National Forest, (928) 333-4301, www.fs.usda.gov/asnf
Finding the campground: From Heber, drive 12 miles west on AZ 260 and turn left onto FR 300. Continue 4 miles to the campground.
About the campground: This small campground is about a mile down the road from the Black Canyon Rim campground. The nearest full services are in Heber.

106 Fool Hollow Lake Recreation Area

Location: About 2 miles east of Show Low, on Fool Hollow Lake
Sites: 123 tent and RV; 31 electric
Road conditions: Paved
Management: Fool Hollow Lake Recreation Area, (928) 537-3680, azstateparks.com/Parks/FOHO; reservations (520) 586-2283, azstateparks.itinio.com
Finding the campground: From the intersection of US 60 and White Mountain Boulevard (AZ 260 east) in Show Low, drive 1.9 miles west on US 60, then turn right on AZ 260 west (toward Payson). Drive 1.9 miles; turn right onto West Old Linden Road. Continue 0.6 mile, then turn left at the sign for Fool Hollow Lake State Park.
About the campground: This large recreation complex in the pines and junipers on the shore of Fool Hollow Lake features a visitor center and hiking trails. The campground has showers and partial hook-ups. The scenic lake is popular with anglers and boaters. Full services are available in Show Low.

107 Show Low Lake

Location: About 5 miles south of Show Low, on Show Low Lake
Sites: 75 tent and RV; some electric hookups
Road conditions: Paved
Management: Show Low Lake County Park, (928) 537-4126, www.campshowlowlake.com; reservations (888) 537-7762, www.campshowlowlake.com
Finding the campground: From East Deuce of Clubs (US 60) and South White Mountain Boulevard (AZ 260 east) in Show Low, drive 3.9 miles south on South White Mountain Boulevard (AZ 260 east), then turn left on Show Low Lake Road and drive 1.0 mile to the campground.

About the campground: Located in the middle of the Show Low–Pinetop–Lakeside community, this campground could hardly be more convenient. Fishing and boating are both available on the lake. Full services are available in Show Low and Pinetop-Lakeside.

108 Lakeside

Location: In Pinetop-Lakeside
Sites: 83 tent and RV up to 32 feet; no hookups
Road conditions: Paved
Management: Apache-Sitgreaves National Forest, (928) 333-4301, www.fs.usda.gov/asnf; reservations (877) 444-6777, www.recreation.gov
Finding the campground: The campground is south of AZ 260, about 9 miles south of Show Low, in the middle of Pinetop-Lakeside.
About the campground: The campground is in the midst of the busy summer resort area of Pinetop-Lakeside, which stretches for miles along the highway. Full services are available in Pinetop-Lakeside.

109 Scott Reservoir

Location: In Pinetop-Lakeside, on Scott Reservoir
Sites: 12 tent
Road conditions: All-weather dirt
Management: Apache-Sitgreaves National Forest, (928) 333-4301, www.fs.usda.gov/asnf
Finding the campground: From Pinetop-Lakeside, drive about 2 miles north on FR 45 to the campground.
About the campground: This small campground is on the west shore of Scott Reservoir on the north side of Pinetop-Lakeside. Full services are available in Pinetop-Lakeside.

110 Los Burros

Location: 25 miles east of Show Low, on the Mogollon Plateau
Sites: 10 tent and RV up to 22 feet; no hookups
Road conditions: Paved, dirt
Management: Apache-Sitgreaves National Forest, (928) 333-4301, www.fs.usda.gov/asnf
Finding the campground: From Show Low, drive 18 miles east on AZ 260 to McNary and turn left onto FR 224. Go 7 miles to the campground.
About the campground: This small, out-of-the-way campground is a good base for exploring the eastern Mogollon Rim country. Mountain bikers can check out the many forest roads. The nearest full services are in Pinetop-Lakeside.

Alpine

The highest of the High Country stretches across the White Mountains, from the town of Springerville to the hamlet of Alpine near the New Mexico boarder and south along the famous Coronado Trail to the old mining towns of Clifton and Morenci. The fir-, spruce-, and aspen-forested mountains are drained by the headwaters of several rivers, including the Little Colorado, the Black, the White, the Blue, and the San Francisco Rivers. These rivers and smaller streams provide some of the state's best stream fishing. And of course there are many mountain lakes, large and small, for boaters and anglers.

Wilderness enthusiasts have much to choose from, including Mount Baldy, Bear Wallow, and Escudilla Wildernesses and the vast Blue Range Primitive Area. Escudilla Mountain was one of the favorite places of Aldo Leopold, the USDA Forest Service ranger who did much to establish the National Wilderness System. And the Blue Range is the site of an experiment to restore the Mexican gray wolf to its native habitat. If you want to explore the White Mountains by vehicle or mountain bike, you have an extensive network of forest roads to choose from—some maintained, some primitive.

Visit Casa Malpais Museum north of Springerville to learn about the mysterious Mogollon people who once lived here. You can trace the route of Spanish explorer Francisco Vasquez de Coronado by driving the Coronado Trail, US 191, from Springerville to Morenci. During the mid-sixteenth century, Coronado led an expedition from Mexico City to explore the northern reaches of what was then New Spain.

For more information:
Greenlee County Chamber of Commerce
66 N. Coronado Blvd.
Clifton, AZ 85523
(928) 965-8154
www.facebook.com/pages/Greenlee-County-Chamber-of-Commerce/1254
78777523286

Springerville–Eagar Round Valley Chamber of Commerce
418 E. Main St.
Springerville, AZ 85938
(928) 333-2123
www.springerville-eagarchamber.com

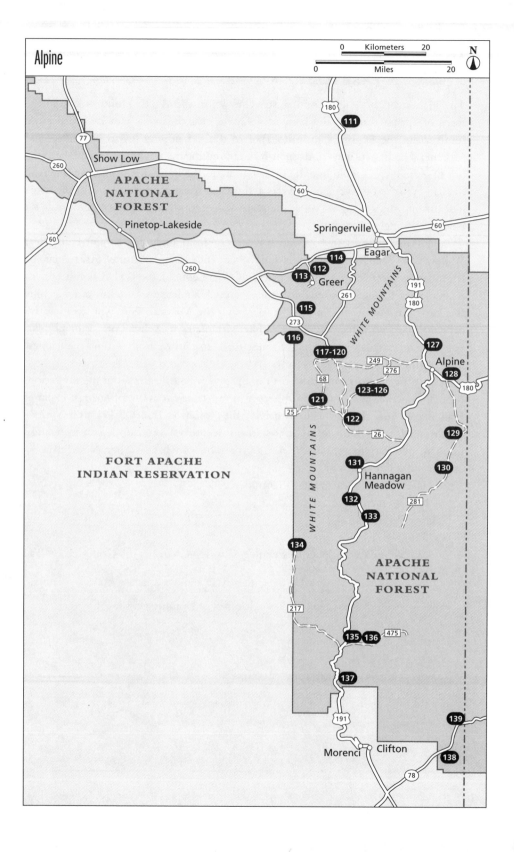

Number	Name	Elevation	Season	RV/Trailer	Sites	Water	RV dump	Fishing	Hiking trails	Boating	Boat launch	Wheelchair access	Fee	Stay limit, days
111	Lyman Lake State Park	6,000	Year-round	•	61	•	•	•		•	•	•	•	14
112	Benney Creek	8,300	May–Sept	•	24	•		•					•	14
113	Rolfe C. Hoyer	8,300	May–Sept	•	91	•	•	•	•			•	•	14
114	South Fork	7,600	Year-round	•	12	•		•	•					14
115	Winn	9,300	May–Oct	•	63	•		•	•			•	•	14
116	Gabaldon	9,400	June–Sept	•	5			•						14
117	Brookchar	9,100	May–Sept		13	•		•	•	•	•	•	•	14
118	Cutthroat	9,100	May–Sept		18	•		•	•	•	•	•	•	14
119	Grayling	9,100	May–Sept	•	23	•		•	•	•	•	•	•	14
120	Rainbow	9,100	May–Sept	•	152	•		•	•	•	•	•	•	14
121	Buffalo Crossing	7,600	May–Oct	•	16	•		•					•	14
122	Horse Spring	7,680	May–Oct	•	27	•		•				•	•	14
123	Raccoon	7,600	May–Oct	•	10	•		•					•	14
124	Deer Creek	7,645	May–Oct	•	6	•		•					•	14
125	Aspen	7,780	May–Oct		6	•		•					•	14
126	Diamond Rock	7,900	May–Oct	•	12	•		•					•	14
127	Alpine Divide	8,500	May–Sept	•	12	•						•	•	14
128	Luna Lake	8,000	May–Sept	•	50	•		•		•	•	•	•	14
129	Upper Blue	6,200	Year-round	•	3			•						14
130	Blue Crossing	6,200	Year-round	•	4			•						14
131	Hannagan	9,100	May–Oct	•	8	•			•					14
132	KP Cienega	9,000	May–Sept	•	5				•					14
133	Strayhorse	8,200	Apr–Nov	•	7	•			•					14
134	Honeymoon	5,600	May–Sept	•	4	•		•						14
135	Upper Juan Miller	5,800	Year-round		4									14
136	Lower Juan Miller	5,700	Year-round	•	4									14
137	Granville	6,600	Apr–Nov	•	11	•								14
138	Black Jack	6,300	Year-round	•	10									14
139	Coal Creek	5,900	Year-round	•	5									14

111 Lyman Lake State Park

Location: About 14 miles north of Springerville, on Lyman Lake
Sites: 61 tent and RV; 38 water and electric hookups, some with sewer
Road conditions: Paved
Management: Lyman Lake State Park, (928) 337-4441, azstateparks.com/Parks/LYLA; reservations (520) 586-2283, azstateparks.itinio.com
Finding the campground: From Springerville, go 13 miles north on US 180; turn right and continue 1 mile to the park.
About the campground: Lyman Lake is a reservoir on the Little Colorado River in the high-desert grasslands of eastern Arizona. It's popular with anglers and boaters. Partial hookups are available, as are showers and a group camping area. Due to the elevation, temperatures are tolerable in summer, although summer weekends are busy. Winter is cold and windy; the best seasons are spring and fall. The nearest full services are in St. Johns and Springerville.

112 Benney Creek

Location: About 15 miles southwest of Springerville, in the White Mountains
Sites: 24 tent and RV up to 24 feet; no hookups
Road conditions: Paved
Management: Apache-Sitgreaves National Forest, (928) 333-4301, www.fs.usda.gov/asnf; reservations (877) 444-6777, www.recreation.gov
Finding the campground: From Springerville, drive 12 miles west on AZ 260 and turn left onto AZ 273. Continue 2.5 miles to the campground on the left.
About the campground: This medium-size campground in the alpine forest near Greer is popular with anglers, who fish nearby Greer Lakes. The campground is a great base for exploring the White Mountains, which has many lakes and streams as well as hiking trails. Limited supplies are available in Greer; the nearest full services are in Eagar and Springerville.

113 Rolfe C. Hoyer

Location: 15 miles southwest of Springerville, in the White Mountains
Sites: 91 tent and RV up to 45 feet; no hookups
Road conditions: Paved
Management: Apache-Sitgreaves National Forest, (928) 333-4301, www.fs.usda.gov/asnf; reservations (877) 444-6777, www.recreation.gov
Finding the campground: From Springerville, drive 12 miles west on AZ 260 and turn left onto AZ 273. Continue 3 miles to the campground on the right.
About the campground: This is the main campground at Greer Lakes. Limited supplies are available in Greer; the nearest full services are in Eagar and Springerville.

114 South Fork

Location: About 10 miles southwest of Springerville, in the White Mountains

Sites: 12 tent and RV up to 32 feet; no hookups

Road conditions: Paved, dirt

Management: Apache-Sitgreaves National Forest, (928) 333-4301, www.fs.usda.gov/asnf

Finding the campground: From Springerville, drive 7 miles west on AZ 260 and turn left onto FR 560. Continue 2.5 miles to the campground.

About the campground: This small, out-of-the-way campground is located on the South Fork Little Colorado River just inside the forest boundary. Trout fishing is popular on the river. The nearest full services are in Eagar and Springerville.

115 Winn

Location: About 30 miles southwest of Springerville, in the White Mountains

Sites: 63 tent and RV up to 40 feet; no hookups

Road conditions: Paved, all-weather dirt

Along the West Fork of the Little Colorado River, near Winn Campground

Management: Apache-Sitgreaves National Forest, (928) 333-4301, www.fs.usda.gov/asnf; reservations (877) 444-6777, www.recreation.gov

Finding the campground: From Springerville, drive 5 miles west on AZ 260 and turn left onto AZ 261. Continue 18 miles; turn right onto AZ 273. Go 6 miles and turn right onto FR 554; continue 1 mile to the campground.

About the campground: This large campground in the White Mountains makes a good base to explore the nearby Mount Baldy Wilderness, which has a network of trails. It's also popular with anglers, who fish for trout in the mountain streams and lakes. A group campground is available. The nearest full services are in Eagar and Springerville.

116 Gabaldon

Location: About 27 miles southwest of Springerville, in the White Mountains
Sites: 5 tent and RV up to 16 feet, with horse corrals
Road conditions: Paved, all-weather dirt
Management: Apache-Sitgreaves National Forest, (928) 333-4301, www.fs.usda.gov/asnf
Finding the campground: From Springerville, drive 5 miles west on AZ 260 and then turn left onto AZ 261. Continue 18 miles; turn right to remain on AZ 273. Go 4 miles to the campground, which is on the left.
About the campground: This small campground is close to several trailheads at the edge of the Mount Baldy Wilderness, so it's popular with hikers and equestrians. The nearest full services are in Eagar and Springerville.

117 Brookchar

Location: 26 miles southwest of Springerville, in the White Mountains at Big Lake
Sites: 13 tent
Road conditions: Paved
Management: Apache-Sitgreaves National Forest, (928) 333-4301, www.fs.usda.gov/asnf; reservations (877) 444-6777, www.recreation.gov
Finding the campground: From Springerville, drive 5 miles west on AZ 260 and turn left onto AZ 261. Continue 18 miles and turn left onto FR 113. Go 2 miles; turn right onto FR 115 and continue 1 mile to the campground.
About the campground: This is one of several small to medium-size campgrounds on the shore of Big Lake. As the name implies, Big Lake is the largest in the White Mountains. This beautiful alpine lake, set in rolling meadows scattered with patches of fir and spruce forests, is understandably popular with boaters and anglers. These campgrounds are best avoided on summer weekends. Fall can be perfect, as the mountainsides are slashed with golden color as the quaking aspens change. Hiking, mountain bike, and nature trails are in the area. Showers are available. The area is closed by large amounts of snow during winter and spring. Limited supplies are available at the lake; the nearest full services are in Eagar and Springerville.

118 Cutthroat

Location: 26 miles southwest of Springerville, in the White Mountains at Big Lake

Sites: 18 tent

Road conditions: Paved

Management: Apache-Sitgreaves National Forest, (928) 333-4301, www.fs.usda.gov/asnf; reservations (877) 444-6777, www.recreation.gov

Finding the campground: From Springerville, drive 5 miles west on AZ 260 and turn left on AZ 261. Continue 18 miles and turn left onto FR 113. Go 2 miles; turn right onto FR 115 and continue 1 mile to the campground.

About the campground: This is another of the small to medium-size campgrounds at Big Lake. Limited supplies are available at the lake; the nearest full services are in Eagar and Springerville.

119 Grayling

Location: 26 miles southwest of Springerville, in the White Mountains at Big Lake

Sites: 23 tent and RV up to 22 feet; no hookups

Road conditions: Paved

Management: Apache-Sitgreaves National Forest, (928) 333-4301, www.fs.usda.gov/asnf; reservations (877) 444-6777, www.recreation.gov

Finding the campground: From Springerville, drive 5 miles west on AZ 260 and turn left onto AZ 261. Continue 18 miles and turn left onto FR 113. Go 2 miles; turn right onto FR 115 and continue 1 mile to the campground.

About the campground: Yet another of several small to medium-size campgrounds on the shore of Big Lake. Limited supplies are available at the lake; the nearest full services are in Eagar and Springerville.

120 Rainbow

Location: 26 miles southwest of Springerville, in the White Mountains at Big Lake

Sites: 152 tent and RV up to 32 feet; no hookups

Road conditions: Paved

Management: Apache-Sitgreaves National Forest, (928) 333-4301, www.fs.usda.gov/asnf; reservations (877) 444-6777, www.recreation.gov

Finding the campground: From Springerville, drive 5 miles west on AZ 260 and turn left onto AZ 261. Continue 18 miles and turn left onto FR 113. Go 2 miles; turn right onto FR 115 and continue 1 mile to the campground.

About the campground: This is the largest campground on the shore of Big Lake. This campground features a nature trail and a seasonal visitor center. The lake is popular with anglers and boaters but also makes a good base for exploring the White Mountains. Limited supplies are available at the lake; the nearest full services are in Eagar and Springerville.

121 Buffalo Crossing

Location: 26 miles southwest of Alpine, in the White Mountains
Sites: 16 tent and RV up to 20 feet; no hookups
Road conditions: Paved, all-weather dirt
Management: Apache-Sitgreaves National Forest, (928) 333-4301, www.fs.usda.gov/asnf
Finding the campground: From Alpine, drive 14 miles south on US 191 and turn right onto FR 26. Continue 9 miles; turn right onto FR 24 and go 3 miles to the campground.
About the campground: This small campground is very popular with anglers because of its location on the East Fork Black River, a trout stream. It's also a good base for exploring the southern part of the White Mountains. Limited services are available in Alpine; full services are available in Eagar and Springerville.

122 Horse Spring

Location: About 28 miles southwest of Alpine, in the White Mountains
Sites: 27 tent and RV up to 32 feet; no hookups
Road conditions: Paved, all-weather dirt
Management: Apache-Sitgreaves National Forest, (928) 333-4301, www.fs.usda.gov/asnf
Finding the campground: From Alpine, drive 2.0 miles north on US 191 to FR 249. Turn left and go 5.0 miles to FR 276. Turn left and follow FR 276 for 6.0 miles to the East Fork Recreation Area.
About the campground: This is a medium-size campground near the Black River. It's a good base for exploring the southern part of the White Mountains, as well as fishing. Limited services are available in Alpine; full services are available in Eagar and Springerville.

123 Raccoon

Location: About 26 miles southwest of Alpine, in the White Mountains
Sites: 10 tent and RV; no hookups
Road conditions: Paved, all-weather dirt
Management: Apache-Sitgreaves National Forest, (928) 333-4301, www.fs.usda.gov/asnf
Finding the campground: From Alpine, drive 2.0 miles north on US 191 to FR 249. Turn left and go 5.0 miles to FR 276. Turn left and follow FR 276 for 6.0 miles to the East Fork Recreation Area.
About the campground: This is a small campground on the East Fork Black River. It's also a good base for exploring the southern part of the White Mountains and for fishing. Limited services are available in Alpine; full services are available in Eagar and Springerville.

124 Deer Creek

Location: About 26 miles southwest of Alpine, in the White Mountains
Sites: 6 tent and RV; no hookups
Road conditions: Paved, all-weather dirt
Management: Apache-Sitgreaves National Forest, (928) 333-4301, www.fs.usda.gov/asnf
Finding the campground: From Alpine, drive 2.0 miles north on US 191 to FR 249. Turn left and go 5.0 miles to FR 276. Turn left and follow FR 276 for 6.0 miles to the East Fork Recreation Area.
About the campground: This is another small campground on the East Fork Black River. It's also a good base for fishing and exploring the southern part of the White Mountains on foot or by vehicle. Limited services are available in Alpine; full services are available in Eagar and Springerville.

125 Aspen

Location: About 26 miles southwest of Alpine, in the White Mountains
Sites: 6 tent
Road conditions: Paved, all-weather dirt
Management: Apache-Sitgreaves National Forest, (928) 333-4301, www.fs.usda.gov/asnf
Finding the campground: From Alpine, drive 2.0 miles north on US 191 to FR 249. Turn left and go 5.0 miles to FR 276. Turn left and follow FR 276 for 6.0 miles to the East Fork Recreation Area.
About the campground: This is yet another small campground on the East Fork Black River. It's also a good base for exploring the southern part of the White Mountains. Limited services are available in Alpine; full services are available in Eagar and Springerville.

126 Diamond Rock

Location: About 26 miles southwest of Alpine, in the White Mountains
Sites: 12 tent and RV up to 10 feet; no hookups
Road conditions: Paved, all-weather dirt
Management: Apache-Sitgreaves National Forest, (928) 333-4301, www.fs.usda.gov/asnf
Finding the campground: From Alpine, drive 2.0 miles north on US 191 to FR 249. Turn left and go 5.0 miles to FR 276. Turn left and follow FR 276 for 6.0 miles to the East Fork Recreation Area.
About the campground: This is another small campground on the East Fork Black River. It's a good base for exploring the southern part of the White Mountains. Limited services are available in Alpine; full services are available in Eagar and Springerville.

Escudilla Mountain, near Alpine Divide Campground

127 Alpine Divide

Location: About 4 miles north of Alpine, in the White Mountains
Sites: 12 tent and RV up to 12 feet; no hookups
Road conditions: Paved
Management: Apache-Sitgreaves National Forest, (928) 333-4301, www.fs.usda.gov/asnf
Finding the campground: From Alpine, drive 4 miles north on US 191. The campground is on the right.
About the campground: This small campground is set in the alpine forest right next to the highway, so it's not only in a beautiful setting, it's convenient as well—but don't expect to find space on a summer weekend. It's a good base for exploring the trails on nearby Escudilla Mountain, the second-highest summit in the White Mountains and one of the highest in the state. Limited services are available in Alpine; full services are available in Eagar and Springerville.

128 Luna Lake

Location: About 6 miles east of Alpine, in the White Mountains
Sites: 50 tent and RV up to 32 feet; no hookups
Road conditions: Paved, all-weather dirt
Management: Apache-Sitgreaves National Forest, (928) 333-4301, www.fs.usda.gov/asnf
Finding the campground: From Alpine, drive 4 miles east on US 180 and turn left onto FR 570. Continue 2 miles to the campground.
About the campground: Luna Lake is a reservoir on the San Francisco River, and the campground is pleasantly located on its northeast shore. A group campground is available by reservation. A wheelchair-accessible fishing dock, picnic area, and restroom are located adjacent to the public boat launch ramp on the south shore of the lake. This is also a good base for exploring the Blue Range Primitive Area to the south. Limited services are available in Alpine; full services are available in Eagar and Springerville.

129 Upper Blue

Location: About 15 miles south of Alpine, on the Blue River
Sites: 3 tent and RV up to 16 feet; no hookups
Road conditions: Paved, all-weather dirt
Management: Apache-Sitgreaves National Forest, (928) 333-4301, www.fs.usda.gov/asnf
Finding the campground: From Alpine, drive 3 miles east on US 180 and turn right onto FR 281. Continue 14 miles to the campground, which is on the right.
About the campground: This tiny campground will mainly be of interest to hikers headed into the nearby Blue Range Primitive Area. Limited services are available in Alpine; full services are available in Eagar and Springerville.

130 Blue Crossing

Location: About 21 miles south of Alpine, on the Blue River
Sites: 4 tent and RV up to 16 feet; no hookups
Road conditions: Paved, dirt
Management: Apache-Sitgreaves National Forest, (928) 333-4301, www.fs.usda.gov/asnf
Finding the campground: From Alpine, drive 3 miles east on US 180 and turn right on FR 281. Continue 20 miles; turn right onto FR 567 and go 0.1 mile to the campground. During high-water events, which are common in spring, the campground may not be accessible.
About the campground: This small campground is mainly of interest to anglers who wish to fish the Blue River as well as backpackers headed into the nearby Blue Range Primitive Area. Limited services are available in Alpine; full services are available in Eagar and Springerville.

131 Hannagan

Location: About 22 miles south of Alpine, in the White Mountains
Sites: 8 tent and RV up to 16 feet; no hookups
Road conditions: Paved
Management: Apache-Sitgreaves National Forest, (928) 333-4301, www.fs.usda.gov/asnf
Finding the campground: From Alpine, drive 23 miles south on US 191. The campground is on the right.
About the campground: This small campground will appeal mainly to backpackers and equestrians headed into the backcountry—either the Bear Wallow Wilderness to the west or the Blue Range Primitive Area just to the east. A livestock corral is available at Hannagan trailhead, 0.5 mile east of the campground. Limited services are available in Hannagan Meadow and in Alpine; full services are available in Eagar and Springerville.

132 KP Cienega

Location: About 26 miles south of Alpine, in the White Mountains
Sites: 5 tent and RV up to 16 feet; no hookups
Road conditions: Paved
Management: Apache-Sitgreaves National Forest, (928) 333-4301, www.fs.usda.gov/asnf
Finding the campground: From Alpine, drive 28 miles south on US 191and turn left onto FR 155. Continue about 2 miles to the campground.
About the campground: This small campground is set at the edge of an alpine meadow at the head of KP Creek. Trails lead into the Blue Range Primitive Area. Limited services are available in Hannagan Meadow and in Alpine; full services are available in Eagar and Springerville.

133 Strayhorse

Location: About 31 miles south of Alpine, along the Coronado Trail, US 191
Sites: 7 tent and RV up to 16 feet; no hookups
Road conditions: Paved
Management: Apache-Sitgreaves National Forest, (928) 333-4301, www.fs.usda.gov/asnf
Finding the campground: From Alpine, drive 31 miles south on US 191 to the campground on the left.
About the campground: This small campground appeals mainly to those who wish to explore the many trails on foot or horse, including routes into the Blue Range Primitive Area and Bear Wallow Wilderness. It's also a convenient stop for those who drive the historic Coronado Trail. Horse corrals are available. Limited services are available in Hannagan Meadow and in Alpine; full services are available in Eagar and Springerville.

134 Honeymoon

Location: About 45 miles north of Clifton, along Eagle Creek
Sites: 4 tent and RV up to 16 feet; no hookups
Road conditions: Paved, dirt
Management: Apache-Sitgreaves National Forest, (928) 333-4301, www.fs.usda.gov/asnf
Finding the campground: From Clifton, drive 25 miles north on US 191 and turn left onto FR 217. Continue 20 miles to the campground.
About the campground: This tiny and remote campground appeals mainly to those who wish to fish and explore the Eagle Creek area. Limited services are available in Clifton; full services are available in Safford.

135 Upper Juan Miller

Location: About 27 miles north of Clifton, near the Coronado Trail, US 191
Sites: 4 tent
Road conditions: Paved, dirt
Management: Apache-Sitgreaves National Forest, (928) 333-4301, www.fs.usda.gov/asnf
Finding the campground: From Clifton, drive 26 miles north on US 191 and turn right onto FR 475. Continue less than a mile to the campground.
About the campground: This is one of two small campgrounds located together near the Coronado Trail. It's a convenient stop for those who drive the historic route and also a good base for those exploring the backcountry. Limited services are available in Clifton; full services are available in Safford.

136 Lower Juan Miller

Location: About 28 miles north of Clifton, near the Coronado Trail, US 191
Sites: 4 tent and RV up to 16 feet; no hookups
Road conditions: Paved, dirt
Management: Apache-Sitgreaves National Forest, (928) 333-4301, www.fs.usda.gov/asnf
Finding the campground: From Clifton, drive 26 miles north on US 191 and turn right onto FR 475. Continue about 1.5 miles to the campground.
About the campground: This is one of two small campgrounds located together near the Coronado Trail. Limited services are available in Clifton; full services are available in Safford.

137 Granville

Location: 18 miles north of Clifton, along the Coronado Trail, US 191
Sites: 11 tent and RV up to 16 feet; no hookups
Road conditions: Paved
Management: Apache-Sitgreaves National Forest, (928) 333-4301, www.fs.usda.gov/asnf
Finding the campground: From Clifton, drive 18 miles north on US 191 to the campground on the right.
About the campground: This is another convenient stop for those exploring the historic Coronado Trail and also a good base for exploring the backcountry. Horse corrals are available. Limited services are available in Clifton; full services are available in Safford.

138 Black Jack

Location: About 23 miles southeast of Clifton, in the Big Lue Mountains
Sites: 10 tent and RV up to 16 feet; no hookups
Road conditions: Paved
Management: Apache-Sitgreaves National Forest, (928) 333-4301, www.fs.usda.gov/asnf
Finding the campground: From Clifton, drive 9 miles south on US 191 and turn left onto AZ 78. Continue about 14 miles to the campground.
About the campground: This small campground appeals mainly to campers passing through on the highway. It can also serve as a base for exploring the Big Lue Mountains. Limited services are available in Clifton; full services are available in Safford.

139 Coal Creek

Location: About 27 miles southeast of Clifton, in the Big Lue Mountains
Sites: 5 tent and RV up to 16 feet; no hookups
Road conditions: Paved
Management: Apache-Sitgreaves National Forest, (928) 333-4301, www.fs.usda.gov/asnf
Finding the campground: From Clifton, drive 9 miles south on US 191 and turn left onto AZ 78. Continue about 18 miles to the campground.
About the campground: This small campground appeals mainly to campers passing through on the highway. It can also serve as a base for exploring the Big Lue Mountains. There are limited services in Clifton; full services are available in Safford.

Old West Country

Old West Country comprises the grassy valleys and high mountains of southeast Arizona. The forested sky islands of the Coronado National Forest are home to a diverse and unique mix of plant and animal species from the Rocky Mountains to the north and the Sierra Madre to the south, in Mexico. Campgrounds abound in the mountains and in the deserts, and there is a wide range of outdoor activities to tempt you, including rock climbing, hiking, fishing, mountain biking, and exploring back roads.

Known as Old West Country because of its rich Western heritage, the region's cultural history started with the Native Americans who made this beautiful area their home. When Europeans entered the area, they soon encountered fierce resistance from the Apache, who hid in the rugged mountains and carried out daring raids on the invaders. Starting in the mid-sixteenth century, Spanish explorers roamed the area and soon made it part of the Spanish Empire in the New World, with Tucson as the capital. The Spanish legacy remains in the form of missions and its deep influence on the culture of the area. After present-day southern Arizona became part of New Mexico Territory in 1853, American cowboys and ranchers began to move into the area, attracted by the rich grasslands. The rate of immigration expanded after Arizona became a separate territory in 1863, and especially after the Civil War ended in 1865. Life on the southern Arizona frontier was complicated by the fierce resistance of the Chiricahua Apache, led by famous chiefs Cochise and Geronimo. Geronimo and his band finally surrendered in 1886, ending the American Indian Wars.

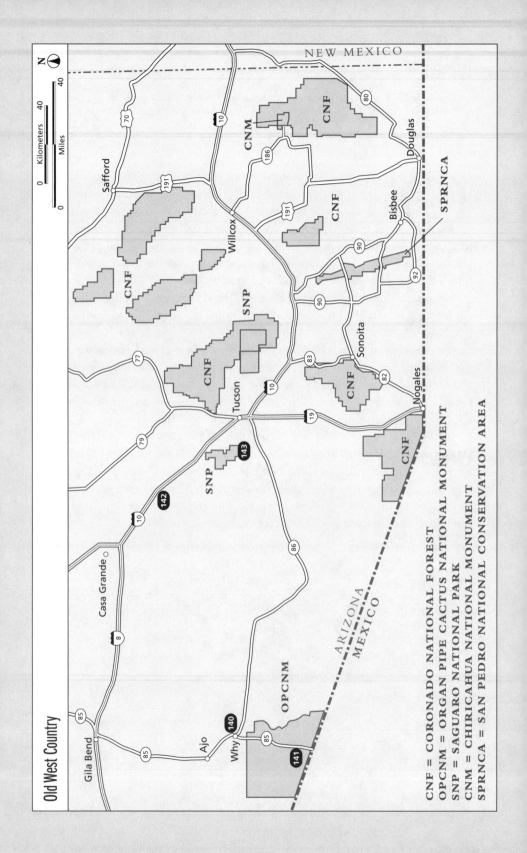

Old West Country

N

0 — Kilometers — 40

0 — Miles — 40

NEW MEXICO

Gila Bend

85

Casa Grande

8

85

Ajo

Why

140

85

141

142

10

143

SNP

79

77

Tucson

10

CNF

SNP

19

86

OPCNM

ARIZONA
MEXICO

Safford

191

70

Willcox

10

191

CNF

SNP

CNM

186

191

CNF

90

90

Sonoita

83

CNF

82

Nogales

CNF

CNF

80

Douglas

Bisbee

90

92

SPRNCA

CNF = CORONADO NATIONAL FOREST
OPCNM = ORGAN PIPE CACTUS NATIONAL MONUMENT
SNP = SAGUARO NATIONAL PARK
CNM = CHIRICAHUA NATIONAL MONUMENT
SPRNCA = SAN PEDRO NATIONAL CONSERVATION AREA

Tucson

Still known as the Old Pueblo, the city of Tucson is the cultural center of southeastern Arizona. This desert city is surrounded by bold mountains that rise dramatically from the beautiful Sonoran Desert foothills to the craggy, forested summits. To the southwest, Organ Pipe Cactus National Monument preserves a unique sample of the Sonoran Desert containing the rare organ pipe cactus and many other unique plants and animals. Closer to the city, Saguaro National Park West in the Tucson Mountains protects one of the finest stands of giant cactus in the Sonoran Desert. Visit the nearby Arizona–Sonora Desert Museum, which has a large and diverse collection of desert plants and animals, many in natural settings. Saguaro National Park East is set in the Rincon Mountains, a chunk of wilderness backcountry that varies from saguaro cactus forest to pine- and fir-covered mountain peaks.

North of Tucson, the Santa Catalina Mountains also range from desert to forest, and you can drive from one to the other in a short time on the Catalina Highway. The road ends near the 9,157-foot summit of Mount Lemmon, site of a summer home

Along one of the many hiking trails in the Tucson Mountains

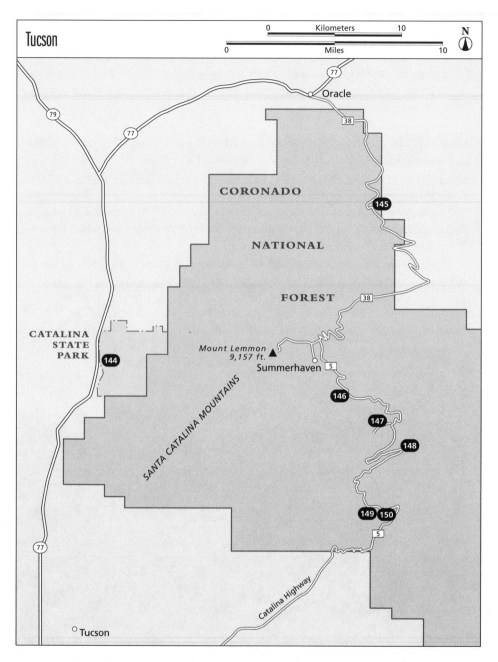

0   Kilometers   10

0   Miles   10

N

Oracle

CORONADO

NATIONAL

FOREST

CATALINA
STATE
PARK

Mount Lemmon
9,157 ft.

Summerhaven

SANTA CATALINA MOUNTAINS

Catalina Highway

Tucson

community and the southernmost alpine ski area in the country. Campgrounds are scattered along the Catalina Highway, as well as in the foothills. Backcountry hikers can spend days exploring the rugged Pusch Ridge and Rincon Wildernesses. The Santa Catalinas are famous among rock climbers for the varied and challenging routes found here.

Tucson has a reputation as the cultural center of Arizona, and you won't be disappointed. You might want to start with the Arizona Historical Society Tucson Museum. Aviation buffs will be in paradise at the Pima Air Museum. If you're a fan of fine photography, don't miss the Center for Creative Photography on the University of Arizona campus, which houses work by such famous photographers as Ansel Adams and Eugene Smith. Children will enjoy the Tucson Children's Museum, which has hands-on exhibits. Want to learn more about the stars? Check out the Flandrau Planetarium, also on campus. It features regular programs on the heavens. You can explore the Spanish history of the area at several sites, including Mission San Xavier del Bac, which has been dubbed the White Dove of the Desert for its classic, white stucco-covered adobe architecture. Tumacacori National Historic Park preserves the remains of another important Spanish mission, and Tubac Presidio State Historic Park preserves an important Spanish military post.

For more information:

Ajo Chamber of Commerce
400 Taladro St.
Ajo, AZ 85321
(520) 387-7742
www.ajochamber.com

Metropolitan Tucson Convention & Visitors Bureau
100 S. Church Ave.
Tucson, AZ 85701
(888) 2-Tucson
www.visittucson.org

Number	Name	Elevation	Season	RV/Trailer	Sites	Water	RV dump	Fishing	Hiking trails	Boating	Boat launch	Wheelchair access	Fee	Stay limit, days
140	Coyote Howls Park	1,780	Year-round	•	600	•	•	•					•	
141	Twin Peaks	1,800	Year-round	•	208	•	•		•			•	•	14
142	Picacho Peak State Park	2,000	Year-round	•	85	•	•		•			•	•	14
143	Gilbert Ray	3,100	Year-round	•	130	•			•				•	7
144	Catalina State Park	2,650	Year-round	•	120		•		•	•		•	•	14
145	Peppersauce	4,700	Year-round	•	17	•						•	•	14
146	Spencer Canyon	8,000	May-Oct	•	60	•						•	•	14
147	Rose Canyon	7,200	Apr-Oct	•	74	•		•	•			•	•	14
148	General Hitchcock	6,000	Year-round		11							•	•	14
149	Gordon Hirabayashi	4,800	Year-round	•	12							•	•	14
150	Molino Basin	4,400	Oct-Apr	•	37			•				•	•	14

140 Coyote Howls Park

Location: About 111 miles west of Tucson, at the town of Why (see map page 130)
Sites: 600 tent and RV; 38 with hookups
Road conditions: Paved
Management: Town of Why, (520) 387-5209, www.coyotehowls.net
Finding the campground: From Tucson, drive 111 miles west on AZ 86 to the town of Why at the junction with AZ 85.
About the campground: This is an alternative to the campground at Organ Pipe Cactus National Monument. Popular with winter visitors, this campground is a good starting point for exploring the national monument and the surrounding Sonoran Desert. Limited services are available in Lukeville, Why, and Ajo; the nearest full services are in Tucson and Phoenix.

141 Twin Peaks

Location: About 130 miles west of Tucson, in Organ Pipe Cactus National Monument (see map page 130)
Sites: 208 tent and RV up to 35 feet; no hookups
Road conditions: Paved
Management: Organ Pipe Cactus National Monument, (520) 387-6849, www.nps.gov/orpi
Finding the campground: From Tucson, drive 111 miles west on AZ 86. Turn left onto AZ 85 at Why and go about 20 miles south. Turn right at the visitor center, and follow the signs to the campground.
About the campground: Popular with winter visitors and travelers, Twin Peaks is located in a unique area of the Sonoran Desert. Nearby activities include scenic drives and hiking trails. The visitor center is a good place to begin exploring the monument. Limited services are available in Lukeville, Why, and Ajo; the nearest full services are in Tucson and Phoenix.

142 Picacho Peak State Park

Location: About 40 miles northwest of Tucson, along I-10 (see map page 130)
Sites: 85 tent and RV; some electric hookups
Road conditions: Paved
Management: Picacho Peak State Park, (520) 466-3183, azstateparks.com/Parks/PIPE
Finding the campground: From Tucson, go 40 miles west on I-10 and exit at Picacho Peak.
About the campground: This desert campground at the base of spectacular Picacho Peak features nature and hiking trails. Showers and some partial hookups are provided. Group camping is available by reservation. Limited services are available nearby; the nearest full services are in Casa Grande and Tucson.

Natural arch at Organ Pipe Cactus National Monument

143 Gilbert Ray

Location: About 10 miles west of Tucson, in the Tucson Mountains (see map page 130)
Sites: 130 tent and RV up to 30 feet; electric hookups
Road conditions: Paved
Management: Tucson Mountain Park, (520) 877-6000, www.pima.gov/nrpr/camping
Finding the campground: From Tucson on I-10, exit at Speedway Boulevard. Go west; the road becomes Gates Pass Road. After 10 miles, turn left into the campground access road.
About the campground: This desert campground is an ideal base from which to explore nearby Saguaro National Park, which has no campgrounds. Summers are too hot here, and not all campground facilities are open then, but fall, winter, and spring are delightful. In wet years the desert becomes a riot of wildflowers in spring. Full services are available in Tucson.

144 Catalina State Park

Location: About 8 miles north of Tucson, at the foot of the Santa Catalina Mountains
Sites: 120 tent and RV; 95 with water and electric hookups
Road conditions: Paved
Management: Catalina State Park, (520) 628-5798, azstateparks.com/Parks/CATA
Finding the campground: From Tucson, drive north on AZ 77. The park is 8 miles north of Ina Road.
About the campground: This is a desert campground and park adjacent to Coronado National Forest. Nature, hiking, and equestrian trails are available in the park and in the national forest. Showers and partial hookups are provided. Equestrian and group facilities are also available. Full services are available in Tucson.

145 Peppersauce

Location: About 38 miles northeast of Tucson, on the northeast slopes of the Santa Catalina Mountains
Sites: 17 tent and RV up to 22 feet; no hookups
Road conditions: Paved, dirt
Management: Coronado National Forest, (520) 388-8300, www.fs.usda.gov/coronado
Finding the campground: From Tucson, drive about 30 miles north on AZ 77 to Oracle. Turn right onto American Avenue (FR 38) and continue 8 miles to the campground.
About the campground: This out-of-the-way campground is located in the northeastern foothills of the Santa Catalina Mountains. Its low elevation keeps the campground open year-round. It's a good base for exploring the remote northern sections of the Catalinas. A small group area is available for up to fifty persons. The nearest services are in Oracle; the nearest full services are in Tucson.

146 Spencer Canyon

Location: About 22 miles northeast of Tucson, in the Santa Catalina Mountains
Sites: 60 tent and RV up to 22 feet; no hookups
Road conditions: Paved
Management: Coronado National Forest, (520) 388-8300, www.fs.usda.gov/coronado
Finding the campground: From Tucson, drive northeast on the Catalina Highway, FR 5, to milepost 21.6; turn left onto the campground access road.
About the campground: Located high in the Santa Catalina Mountains in pine forest, this is one of several mountain campgrounds that provide a cool retreat from the desert below. It's also a good base for exploring the mountains, including the nearby Pusch Ridge Wilderness. Expect the campground to fill rapidly on summer weekends. There are two group areas that accommodate fifteen persons each. More group camping is available at Showers Point Group Campground, about 2 miles to the south. Limited services are available in Summerhaven; the nearest full services are in Tucson.

The Santa Catalina front range above Catalina State Pa

147 Rose Canyon

Location: About 16 miles northeast of Tucson, in the Santa Catalina Mountains
Sites: 74 tent and RV up to 22 feet; no hookups
Road conditions: Paved
Management: Coronado National Forest, (520) 388-8300, www.fs.usda.gov/coronado
Finding the campground: From Tucson, drive northeast on the Catalina Highway, FR 5, to milepost 16. Turn left onto FR 9, the campground access road.
About the campground: This is the largest of several mountain campgrounds that provide a cool retreat from the desert below. Fishing is available in nearby Rose Canyon Lake. Expect the campground to fill rapidly on summer weekends. Limited services are available in Summerhaven; the nearest full services are in Tucson.

148 General Hitchcock

Location: About 12 miles northeast of Tucson, in the Santa Catalina Mountains
Sites: 11 tent
Road conditions: Paved
Management: Coronado National Forest, (520) 388-8300, www.fs.usda.gov/coronado
Finding the campground: From Tucson, drive northeast on the Catalina Highway, FR 5, to milepost 12. Turn right onto FR 605, the campground access road.
About the campground: This is the smallest of the Santa Catalina Mountains campgrounds. It has mostly walk-in tent campsites; trailers and RVs are not allowed. Expect the campground to fill rapidly on summer weekends. Limited services are available in Summerhaven; the nearest full services are in Tucson.

149 Gordon Hirabayashi

Location: About 7 miles northeast of Tucson, in the Santa Catalina Mountains
Sites: 12 tent and RV up to 22 feet; no hookups
Road conditions: Paved
Management: Coronado National Forest, (520) 388-8300, www.fs.usda.gov/coronado
Finding the campground: From Tucson, drive northeast on the Catalina Highway, FR 5, to milepost 7 and the campground on the left.
About the campground: Only slightly higher than Molino Basin Campground, this small site is also hot in summer. It's best enjoyed in fall, winter, and spring. Full services are available in Tucson.

150 Molino Basin

Location: About 6 miles northeast of Tucson, in the Santa Catalina Mountains
Sites: 37 tent and RV up to 22 feet; no hookups
Road conditions: Paved
Management: Coronado National Forest, (520) 388-8300, www.fs.usda.gov/coronado
Finding the campground: From Tucson, drive northeast on the Catalina Highway, FR 5, to Milepost 6; turn left onto the campground access road.
About the campground: This is the lowest in elevation of the Santa Catalina campgrounds, and it's best in fall, winter, and spring. Full services are available in Tucson.

Safford

Safford is the center of a thriving ranching community along the Gila River Valley. Towering above the valley, the Pinaleno Mountains and several smaller ranges are the recreational center of the area. Capped by 10,717-foot Mount Graham, the Pinalenos are more than 50 miles long. The summit ridge and north slopes are covered with a dense, cool forest of pine, fir, oak, and aspen. Campgrounds are scattered along the Swift Trail, a part-paved and part-dirt road that winds along the high south slopes of the range. There are miles of hiking trails, including the rugged Round the Mountain Trail, and several fishing streams. Other backcountry areas to explore include the wild Santa Teresa and Galiuro Mountains, both included in wilderness areas. In the foothills of the Galiuros, beautiful Aravaipa Canyon winds through green streamside trees. Although outdoor recreation is the main activity for campers, you might want to check out Discovery Park, Safford's 165-acre science and cultural center.

Mainly found in Mexico, ocelots are occasionally spotted in southern Arizona

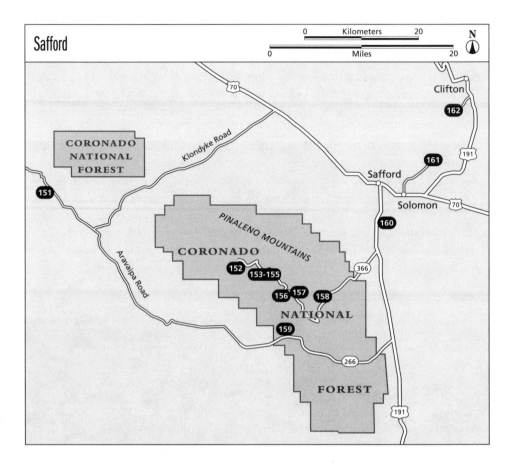

For more information:
Graham County Chamber of Commerce
1111 Thatcher Blvd.
Safford, AZ 85546
(888) 837-1841
www.graham-chamber.com

Number	Name	Elevation	Season	RV/Trailer	Sites	Water	RV dump	Fishing	Hiking trails	Boating	Boat launch	Wheelchair access	Fee	Stay limit, days
151	Fourmile Canyon	3,500	Year-round	•	10	•							•	14
152	Riggs Flat	8,600	Apr–Nov	•	31			•	•			•	•	14
153	Columbine Corrals	9,600	May–Oct	•	6				•				•	14
154	Cunningham	9,000	Apr–Oct	•	10				•			•	•	14
155	Soldier Creek	9,300	Apr–Nov	•	12								•	14
156	Hospital Flat	9,000	Apr–Nov	•	10	•							•	14
157	Shannon	9,100	Apr–Oct	•	11		•	•					•	14
158	Arcadia	6,700	Year-round	•	19				•				•	14
159	Stockton Pass	5,700	Year-round	•	7				•					14
160	Roper Lake State Park	3,130	Year-round	•	100	•		•	•	•	•	•	•	14
161	Riverview	3,100	Year-round		13	•			•			•	•	14
162	Owl Creek	3,100	Year-round		7			•				•	•	14

151 Fourmile Canyon

Location: About 47 miles west of Safford, in the foothills of the Galiuro Mountains
Sites: 10 tent and RV up to 30 feet; no hookups
Road conditions: Paved, all-weather dirt
Management: Bureau of Land Management, (928) 718-3700, www.blm.gov/az
Finding the campground: From Safford, drive west 13.4 miles on US 70; turn left onto Klondyke Road. Continue 32.4 miles to Klondyke; turn left onto Fourmile Canyon Road and go 0.5 mile to the campground.
About the campground: This desert campground is a good retreat during the cooler months of fall, winter, and spring. It's also a good base for exploring the nearby Santa Teresa, Galiuro, and Aravaipa Canyon Wildernesses. The nearest full services are in Safford.

152 Riggs Flat

Location: About 41 miles southwest of Safford, in the Pinaleno Mountains
Sites: 31 tent and RV up to 22 feet; no hookups
Road conditions: Paved, dirt
Management: Coronado National Forest, (520) 388-8300, www.fs.usda.gov/coronado
Finding the campground: From Safford, drive 9 miles south on US 191. Turn right onto Swift Trail, AZ 366, and continue about 32 miles to the campground on the left.

About the campground: Located in the pine and fir forest at the west end of the Swift Trail, this popular spot is the most distant of the Pinaleno campgrounds. Fishing and limited boating are available on nearby Riggs Lake. This is also a good base for exploring the mountains; there are numerous hiking trails in the area. The nearest full services are in Safford.

153 Columbine Corrals

Location: About 40 miles southwest of Safford, in the Pinaleno Mountains
Sites: 6 tent and RV up to 16 feet; no hookups
Road conditions: Paved, dirt
Management: Coronado National Forest, (520) 388-8300, www.fs.usda.gov/coronado
Finding the campground: From Safford, drive 9 miles south on US 191. Turn right onto Swift Trail, AZ 366, and continue about 30 miles to the campground.
About the campground: Located in the pine and fir forest near the town site of old Columbine, this is an equestrian camp with horse facilities and access to trails. The nearest full services are in Safford.

154 Cunningham

Location: About 40 miles southwest of Safford, in the Pinaleno Mountains
Sites: 10 tent and RV up to 22 feet; no hookups
Road conditions: Paved, dirt **Management:** Coronado National Forest, (520) 388-8300, www.fs.usda.gov/coronado
Finding the campground: From Safford, drive 9 miles south on US 191. Turn right on Swift Trail, AZ 366, continue 26.0 miles to the campground.
About the campground: This is another equestrian camp with horse facilities and access to trails, located along the Swift Trail. The nearest full services are in Safford.

155 Soldier Creek

Location: About 37 miles southwest of Safford, in the Pinaleno Mountains
Sites: 12 tent and RV up to 22 feet; no hookups
Road conditions: Paved, dirt
Management: Coronado National Forest, (520) 388-8300, www.fs.usda.gov/coronado
Finding the campground: From Safford, drive 9 miles south on US 191. Turn right onto Swift Trail, AZ 366, and continue about 30 miles to the campground, which is on the left.
About the campground: This is another campground along the Swift Trail in the old Columbine area. It is a good base for exploring the mountains and the numerous hiking trails in the area. The nearest full services are in Safford.

156 Hospital Flat

Location: About 31 miles southwest of Safford, in the Pinaleno Mountains
Sites: 10 tent
Road conditions: Paved, dirt
Management: Coronado National Forest, (520) 388-8300, www.fs.usda.gov/coronado
Finding the campground: From Safford, drive 9 miles south on US 191. Turn right onto Swift Trail, AZ 366, and continue about 23 miles to the campground, which is on the left.
About the campground: This is another small campground along the Swift Trail. This one allows tents only; it is not suitable for trailers and RVs. The nearest full services are in Safford.

157 Shannon

Location: About 30 miles southwest of Safford, in the Pinaleno Mountains
Sites: 11 tent and RV up to 16 feet; no hookups
Road conditions: Paved, dirt
Management: Coronado National Forest, (520) 388-8300, www.fs.usda.gov/coronado
Finding the campground: From Safford, drive 9 miles south on US 191. Turn right onto Swift Trail, AZ 366, and continue 21.8 miles to the campground, which is on the right.
About the campground: This is yet another small campground along the Swift Trail. The nearest full services are in Safford.

Round the Mountain Trailhead, Pinaleno Mountains

158 Arcadia

Location: About 19 miles southwest of Safford, in the Pinaleno Mountains
Sites: 19 tent and RV up to 22 feet; no hookups
Road conditions: Paved
Management: Coronado National Forest, (520) 388-8300, www.fs.usda.gov/coronado
Finding the campground: From Safford, drive 9 miles south on US 191. Turn right onto Swift Trail, AZ 366, and continue about 10 miles to the campground, which is on the right.
About the campground: This is the lowest of the campgrounds along the Swift Trail in the Pinaleno Mountains, and the only one open year-round. Water is available May through October. The nearest full services are in Safford.

159 Stockton Pass

Location: About 25 miles southwest of Safford
Sites: 7 tent and RV up to 22 feet; no hookups
Road conditions: Paved, dirt
Management: Coronado National Forest, (520) 388-8300, www.fs.usda.gov/coronado
Finding the campground: From Safford, drive 17 miles south on US 191. Turn right onto AZ 266, and continue 12 miles to the campground, on the right.
About the campground: Located in the oak woodland on the south slopes of the Pinaleno Mountains, this campground is also the trailhead for the Shake Trail, which climbs north to the Swift Trail, AZ 366. The nearest full services are in Safford.

160 Roper Lake State Park

Location: About 4 miles south of Safford, at Roper Lake
Sites: 100 tent and RV; 45 water and electric hookups
Road conditions: Paved
Management: Roper Lake State Park, (928) 428-6760, azstateparks.com/Parks/ROLA; reservations (520) 586-2283, azstateparks.itinio.com
Finding the campground: From Safford, go about 4 miles south on US 191; turn left into the park.
About the campground: Although summers are hot here, the park is usually busy on summer weekends. Fishing and boating (electric motors only) are popular on the lake. Partial hookups are available, as are showers and a group campsite. Full services are available in Safford.

161 Riverview

Location: About 20 miles northeast of Safford, in the Gila Box Riparian National Conservation Area

Sites: 13 tent

Road conditions: Dirt

Management: Bureau of Land Management, (928) 718-3700, www.blm.gov/az

Finding the campground: From Safford, drive 5 miles east on US 70 to the town of Solomon. Turn left onto Sanchez Road and drive north across the Gila River bridge. Continue 7 miles to the sign for the Gila Box Riparian National Conservation Area. Turn left and drive about 3 miles to the entry sign and the campground.

About the campground: This small campground is a great base for exploring the Gila Box. Bonita Creek and the Gila River both offer lush streamsides populated with cottonwoods, sycamores, and willows. Cliff dwellings, historic homesteads, bighorn sheep, and more than 200 species of birds are among the attractions. The nearest full services are in Safford.

162 Owl Creek

Location: About 10 miles south of Clifton, in the Gila Box Riparian National Conservation Area

Sites: 7 tent

Road conditions: Dirt

Management: Bureau of Land Management, (928) 718-3700, www.blm.gov/az

Finding the campground: From Clifton, drive 4 miles south on US 191. Turn right onto the Black Hills Back Country Byway, and continue 4 miles to the Gila River and the campground.

About the campground: This small campground is a good base for exploring the east end of the Gila Box. The nearest full services are in Clifton.

Nogales

Nogales is best known as the entrance to Mexico and the city of Nogales, Sonora. But campers and recreationists have opportunities here, too. The beautiful grass and oak uplands of the Atacosa Mountains offer plenty of opportunities for back road explorations, as well as a lake very popular with anglers. Hikers will want to check out Sycamore Canyon in the Pajarita Wilderness. Classic ranching country surrounds the hamlets of Patagonia and Sonoita. Anglers and boaters have Patagonia Lake, and hikers can spend days in the Mount Wrightson Wilderness high atop the Santa Rita Mountains. If you're a bird-watcher, you'll want to visit the Patagonia–Sonoita Creek Preserve, maintained by the Nature Conservancy. This world-famous sanctuary, on a major migration route, hosts more than 250 species of birds, including nine varieties of hummingbirds.

For more information:

Nogales/Santa Cruz Chamber of Commerce

123 W. Kino Park

Nogales, AZ 85621

(520) 287-3685

www.thenogaleschamber.com

Pararita Mountains

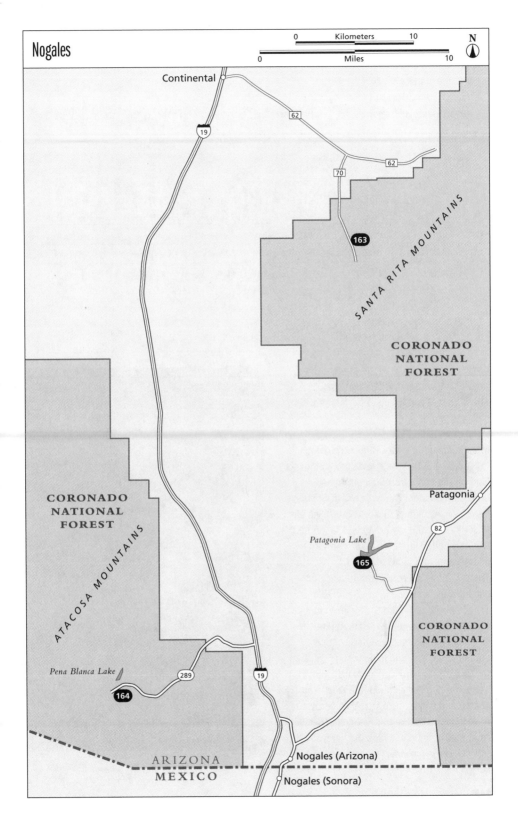

Nogales

Patagonia Area Business Association
307 McKeown Ave.
Patagonia, AZ 85624
(888) 794-0060
www.patagoniaaz.com

Number	Name	Elevation	Season	RV/Trailer	Sites	Water	RV dump	Fishing	Hiking trails	Boating	Boat launch	Wheelchair access	Fee	Stay limit, days
163	Bog Springs	5,200	Year-round	•	13	•			•				•	14
164	White Rock	4,000	Year-round	•	15			•		•	•	•	•	14
165	Patagonia Lake State Park	4,000	Year-round	•	105	•	•	•	•	•	•	•	•	14

163 Bog Springs

Location: About 50 miles northeast of Nogales, in the Santa Rita Mountains
Sites: 13 tent and RV up to 22 feet; no hookups
Road conditions: Paved
Management: Coronado National Forest, (520) 388-8300, www.fs.usda.gov/coronado
Finding the campground: From Nogales, drive 40 miles north on I-19; exit at Continental, 23 miles south of Tucson. Go 6 miles east on FR 62 and turn right onto FR 70, Madera Canyon Road. Continue 4 miles and turn left on the campground access road.
About the campground: This small campground is the only one in the Santa Rita Mountains. Because of its low elevation, the campground is open year-round. It tends to fill quickly on summer weekends. Madera Canyon is famous among birders for its rare species. The canyon is also popular with hikers who want to climb Mount Wrightson or explore the Mount Wrightson Wilderness. There is also a nature trail. Limited services are available in Continental; the nearest full services are in Tucson.

Madera Creek near Bog Springs Campground

164 White Rock

Location: About 16 miles northwest of Nogales, in the Atacosa Mountains
Sites: 15 tent and RV up to 22 feet; no hookups
Road conditions: Paved
Management: Coronado National Forest, (520) 388-8300, www.fs.usda.gov/coronado
Finding the campground: From Nogales, drive 7 miles north on I-19. Turn left on AZ 289 and continue 9 miles west to the campground.
About the campground: This small campground is located near Pena Blanca Lake. The lake is popular with anglers, although the campground is also a good base to explore the Atacosa Mountains, including the Pajarita Wilderness to the west. The nearest full services are in Nogales.

165 Patagonia Lake State Park

Location: About 16 miles northeast of Nogales, on Patagonia Lake
Sites: 105 tent and RV up to 35 feet, with water and electric hookups
Road conditions: Paved
Management: Patagonia Lake State Park, (520) 287-6965, azstateparks.com/Parks/PALA; reservations (520) 586-2283, azstateparks.itinio.com
Finding the campground: From Nogales, drive 12 miles north on AZ 82. Turn left onto Patagonia Lake Road and continue about 4 miles to the park.
About the campground: Located in the scenic oak and grassland country of south-central Arizona, this park is popular year-round. Boating and fishing are very popular on the lake, and weekends are crowded. The park also has hiking trails. On weekdays you can enjoy peaceful sunsets and watch the graceful herons. The campground has showers and a group camping area. Partial hookups are also available. Limited supplies are available in the park and in Patagonia; the nearest full services are in Nogales.

Sierra Vista

Sierra Vista is a retirement and military community at the base of the Huachuca Mountains. Nearby Fort Huachuca was originally established as an army post during the Apache wars and now serves as a test site. The fort's museum traces the history of the "Buffalo Soldiers." Parker Canyon Lake, in the Canelo Hills west of the Huachuca Mountains, is popular with boaters and anglers. The Huachucas, in the Coronado National Forest, run northwest to southeast and culminate in 9,466-foot Miller Peak. The Miller Peak Wilderness is laced with hiking trails, and the Nature Conservancy's Ramsey Canyon Preserve is a legendary site for spotting rare birds. Muleshoe Ranch Preserve, another Nature Conservancy preserve, operated in cooperation with the Bureau of Land Management's San Pedro Riparian National Conservation Area, protects one of the last free-flowing rivers in the state.

For more information:

Sierra Vista Chamber of Commerce

21 E. Willcox Dr.

Sierra Vista, AZ 85635

(520) 458-6940

www.sierravistachamber.org

Number	Name	Elevation	Season	RV/Trailer	Sites	Water	RV dump	Fishing	Hiking trails	Boating	Boat launch	Wheelchair access	Fee	Stay limit, days
166	Lakeview	5,400	Year-round	•	65	•		•	•	•	•	•	•	14
167	Reef Townsite	7,200	Apr–Nov	•	14				•			•	•	14
168	Ramsey Vista	7,400	Apr–Nov	•	8				•			•	•	14

166 Lakeview

Location: About 28 miles southeast of Sonoita, at Parker Lake
Road conditions: Paved, dirt
Sites: 65 tent and RV up to 32 feet; no hookups
Management: Coronado National Forest, (520) 388-8300, www.fs.usda.gov/coronado
Finding the campground: From Sonoita, drive 28 miles south and east on AZ 83 to the campground.
About the campground: This campground is on the east shore of Parker Lake, a small reservoir. It's popular with boaters and anglers. Though it's open year-round, summer weekends tend to be busy. Limited services are available in Sonoita; the nearest full services are in Tucson and Sierra Vista.

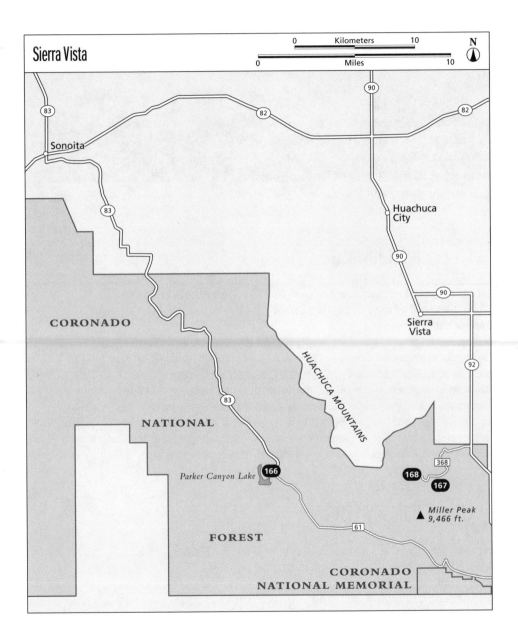

Sierra Vista

Gila monsters appear sluggish but can move fast and deliver a painful, poisonous bite if disturbed.

167 Reef Townsite

Location: About 14 miles southeast of Sierra Vista, in the Huachuca Mountains
Sites: 14 tent and RV up to 12 feet; no hookups
Road conditions: Paved, dirt
Management: Coronado National Forest, (520) 388-8300, www.fs.usda.gov/coronado
Finding the campground: From Sierra Vista at the junction of AZ 90 and AZ 92, drive 7 miles south on AZ 92. Turn right onto Carr Canyon Road, FR 368, and continue 6.5 miles.
About the campground: Located high in the Huachuca Mountains near the old Reef Townsite, this campground is 2,500 feet higher than Sierra Vista and is correspondingly cooler. The view of the surrounding mountains is superb, partially because a series of forest fires have burned many of the large trees in the basin. The campground is a good base for exploring trails into the nearby Miller Peak Wilderness. A group campground is available. The nearest full services are in Sierra Vista.

168 Ramsey Vista

Location: About 14 miles southeast of Sierra Vista, in the Huachuca Mountains
Sites: 8 tent and RV up to 12 feet; no hookups
Road conditions: Paved, dirt
Management: Coronado National Forest, (520) 388-8300, www.fs.usda.gov/coronado
Finding the campground: From Sierra Vista at the junction of AZ 90 and AZ 92, drive 7 miles south on AZ 92. Turn right onto Carr Canyon Road, FR 368, and continue 7 miles to the end of the road.
About the campground: See Reef Townsite campground for details on this area. This campground has horse corrals. The nearest full services are in Sierra Vista.

Douglas

Douglas, in the southeastern corner of the state on the Mexican border; Willcox to the north; and Bisbee to the west frame several sky island mountain ranges with plenty of camping and recreational activities. Cochise Stronghold in the granite-cragged Dragoon Mountains was the last holdout of the famous Chiricahua Apache leader, Cochise, and his band of warriors and their families. The Chiricahua Mountains, a 9,000-foot range crowned with a Rocky Mountain forest of pine and fir, features the Chiricahua Wilderness and many miles of wilderness trails. The north end of the range features stone hoodoos—a wonderland of volcanic rock—protected in Chiricahua National Monument. Nearby Fort Bowie was a post for army soldiers engaged in the desperate fight against the Apache in the nineteenth century.

Western history fans have to visit Tombstone, "the town too tough to die." One of the rowdiest of western mining towns, it was the scene of the famous shootout at the OK Corral, where well-known and obscure gunslingers faced off, guns blazing. The losers died with their boots on and were buried in nearby Boot Hill.

For more information:

Douglas Chamber of Commerce

www.douglasazchamber.org

Hoodoos near Bonita Campground, Chiricahua National Monument

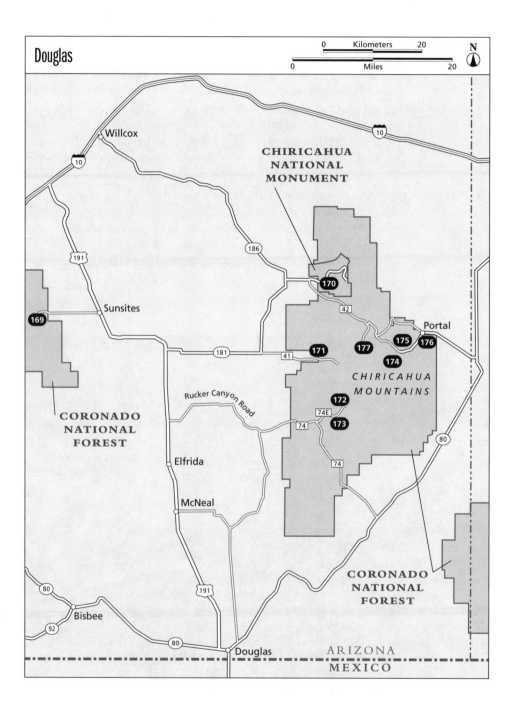

Douglas

Kilometers 20
0
Miles 20

N

Willcox

CHIRICAHUA
NATIONAL
MONUMENT

10

191

Sunsites

169

181

41

171

177

175

176

Portal

174

CHIRICAHUA
MOUNTAINS

170

42

186

Rucker Canyon Road

CORONADO
NATIONAL
FOREST

172

74E

74

173

80

Elfrida

McNeal

74

191

80

CORONADO
NATIONAL
FOREST

Bisbee

92

80

Douglas

ARIZONA

MEXICO

Tombstone Chamber of Commerce
109 S. Fourth St.
PO Box 995
Tombstone, AZ 85638
(888) 457-3929
www.tombstonechamber.com

Willcox Chamber of Commerce
1500 N. Circle I Rd.
Willcox, AZ 85643
(520) 384-2272; (800) 200-2272
www.willcoxchamber.com

Number	Name	Elevation	Season	RV/Trailer	Sites	Water	RV dump	Fishing	Hiking trails	Boating	Boat launch	Wheelchair access	Fee	Stay limit, days
169	Cochise Stronghold	5,000	Sept-May	•	12				•				•	14
170	Bonita	5,400	Year-round	•	22	•			•				•	14
171	Sycamore	6,200	Year-round	•	7				•				•	14
172	Rucker Forest Camp	6,500	Mar-Oct	•	13				•				•	14
173	Cypress Park	6,000	Mar-Oct	•	7				•				•	14
174	Sunny Flat	5,200	Year-round	•	13				•				•	14
175	Stewart	5,100	Apr-Oct	•	6	•			•				•	14
176	Idlewilde	5,000	Apr-Sept	•	9	•			•				•	14
177	Rustler Park	8,500	Apr-Nov	•	22				•				•	14

169 Cochise Stronghold

Location: About 57 miles northwest of Douglas, in the Dragoon Mountains
Sites: 12 tent and RV up to 22 feet; no hookups
Road conditions: Paved, dirt
Management: Coronado National Forest, (520) 388-8300, www.fs.usda.gov/coronado
Finding the campground: From Douglas, drive west 2 miles on AZ 80. Turn right onto US 191 and continue 46 miles to Sunsites. Turn left onto Ironwood Road, which becomes FR 84. Go 9 miles to the road's end.
About the campground: This surprising spot, tucked away in a side canyon of the Dragoon Mountains, is dramatically set in Stronghold Canyon East amid shady oaks. There is a nature trail, and a hiking trail leads over Stronghold Pass to Stronghold Canyon West. For many years this area was the hideout of Cochise, the famous Chiricahua Apache chief, and his loyal followers. Limited services are available in Sunsites; the nearest full services are in Willcox and Douglas.

170 Bonita

Location: About 37 miles southeast of Willcox, in the Chiricahua Mountains
Sites: 22 tent and RV up to 29 feet; no hookups
Road conditions: Paved
Management: Chiricahua National Monument, (520) 824-3560, www.nps.gov/chir
Finding the campground: From Willcox, drive 31 miles southeast on AZ 186 and turn left onto AZ 181. Continue into Chiricahua National Monument and go 6 miles to the monument headquarters and the campground.
About the campground: This pleasant campground, set in piñon pines, junipers, and oaks at the bottom of Bonita Canyon in Chiricahua National Monument, is a great base for exploration of the monument. A scenic drive and miles of hiking trails wind through weird stone hoodoos. The nearest full services are in Willcox.

171 Sycamore

Location: About 51 miles southeast of Willcox, in the Chiricahua Mountains
Sites: 7 tent and RV up to 22 feet; no hookups
Road conditions: Paved, dirt
Management: Coronado National Forest, (520) 388-8300, www.fs.usda.gov/coronado
Finding the campground: From Willcox, drive 31 miles southeast on AZ 186 and go straight on AZ 181. Continue 10 miles; turn left onto West Turkey Creek Road, which becomes FR 41. Go 10 miles to the campground. **About the campground:** Another small campground on the west side of the Chiricahua Mountains, it's primarily of interest to hikers headed for the nearby high country in the Chiricahua Wilderness. The nearest full services are in Willcox.

172 Rucker Forest Camp

Location: About 60 miles north of Douglas, in the Chiricahua Mountains
Sites: 13 tent and RV up to 16 feet; no hookups
Road conditions: Paved, dirt
Management: Coronado National Forest, (520) 388-8300, www.fs.usda.gov/coronado
Finding the campground: From Douglas, drive west 2 miles on AZ 80 and turn right onto US 191. Continue 31 miles and turn right onto Rucker Canyon Road. Continue 22 miles; turn left onto FR 74E and go 5 miles to the campground.
About the campground: This is the largest of several small campgrounds in the Rucker Canyon area. Aside from being a cool mountain retreat, Rucker Canyon also has several trailheads for trails into the Chiricahua Wilderness. Limited services are available in Elfrida; the nearest full services are in Douglas.

Big Balanced Rock in Chiricahua National Monument

Chiricahua Mountains near Sunny Flat Campground

173 Cypress Park

Location: About 60 miles north of Douglas, in the Chiricahua Mountains
Sites: 7 tent and RV up to 16 feet; no hookups
Road conditions: Paved, dirt
Management: Coronado National Forest, (520) 388-8300, www.fs.usda.gov/coronado
Finding the campground: From Douglas, drive west 2 miles on AZ 80 and turn right onto US 191. Continue 31 miles and turn right onto Rucker Canyon Road. Continue 22 miles; turn left onto FR 74E and go 4 miles to the campground.
About the campground: This is the smallest of several small campgrounds in the Rucker Canyon area. Limited services are available in Elfrida; the nearest full services are in Douglas.

174 Sunny Flat

Location: About 59 miles northeast of Douglas, in the Chiricahua Mountains
Sites: 13 tent and RV up to 16 feet; no hookups
Road conditions: Paved
Management: Coronado National Forest, (520) 388-8300, www.fs.usda.gov/coronado
Finding the campground: From Douglas, drive 49 miles northeast on AZ 80 and turn left onto Portal Road. Continue 10 miles; turn right to remain on FR 42. Turn right again into the campground.
About the campground: This small campground is located below the dramatic cliffs in the Portal area on the east side of the Chiricahua Mountains. The campground is set along a meadow, which has excellent views of the surrounding cliff-bound canyons. Several trails lead into the Chiricahua

Wilderness and connect with an extensive backcountry trail system. Limited supplies are available in Portal; the nearest full services are in Douglas.

175 Stewart

Location: About 58 miles northeast of Douglas, in the Chiricahua Mountains
Sites: 6 tent and RV up to 22 feet; no hookups
Road conditions: Paved
Management: Coronado National Forest, (520) 388-8300, www.fs.usda.gov/coronado
Finding the campground: From Douglas, drive 49 miles northeast on AZ 80 and turn left onto Portal Road. Continue 9 miles to the campground, which is on the left.
About the campground: This is the smallest of the campgrounds in the Portal area. Limited supplies are available in Portal; the nearest full services are in Douglas.

176 Idlewilde

Location: About 58 miles northeast of Douglas, in the Chiricahua Mountains
Sites: 9 tent and RV up to 16 feet; no hookups
Road conditions: Paved
Management: Coronado National Forest, (520) 388-8300, www.fs.usda.gov/coronado
Finding the campground: From Douglas, drive 49 miles northeast on AZ 80 and turn left onto Portal Road. Continue 8.7 miles to the campground, which is on the left.
About the campground: This is the largest and lowest elevation campground in the Portal area. A nature trail is located at the nearby ranger station. Limited supplies are available in Portal; the nearest full services are in Douglas.

177 Rustler Park

Location: About 70 miles northeast of Douglas, in the Chiricahua Mountains
Sites: 22 tent and RV up to 22 feet; no hookups
Road conditions: Paved, dirt
Management: Coronado National Forest, (520) 388-8300, www.fs.usda.gov/coronado
Finding the campground: From Douglas, drive 49 miles northeast on AZ 80 and turn left onto Portal Road. Continue 10 miles; turn right to remain on FR 42. Go 2 miles and stay right again to remain on FR 42. Continue about 6 miles to Onion Saddle and turn left onto FR 42D, the Rustler Park Road. Go 2 miles to the campground.
About the campground: This is an out-of-the-way campground high in the Chiricahua Mountains. It's a good base for those hiking in the Chiricahua Wilderness from the nearby Rustler Park trailhead. The nearest full services are in Willcox.

Organ pipe cactus grows in northern Sonora, Mexico, and extreme southern Arizona, in Old West Country.

Camping Checklist

Use this list as a starting point to remind you what to take on your camping adventure.

Camping Gear

- ❏ camp shoes
- ❏ sleeping bag
- ❏ foam sleeping pad
- ❏ tent
- ❏ ground sheet
- ❏ tarp
- ❏ nylon cord
- ❏ tent pegs
- ❏ first aid kit
- ❏ knife
- ❏ water bottles/containers
- ❏ headlamp
- ❏ extra batteries
- ❏ toilet paper
- ❏ insect repellent
- ❏ rain gear
- ❏ sun hat
- ❏ sun screen
- ❏ lip balm
- ❏ toiletries
- ❏ cooler
- ❏ lantern
- ❏ camp chairs
- ❏ camp table
- ❏ stove
- ❏ fuel
- ❏ cooking pots
- ❏ camp plates, bowls, cups
- ❏ utensils
- ❏ lighter
- ❏ trash bags
- ❏ field guides
- ❏ binoculars
- ❏ camera
- ❏ games

Car

Since many Arizona campgrounds are located in remote areas miles from the nearest town, you should consider carrying these items.

- ❏ jumper cables
- ❏ tools
- ❏ extra water
- ❏ extra food
- ❏ hiking boots
- ❏ day pack
- ❏ maps
- ❏ compass
- ❏ GPS receiver
- ❏ car charger for mobile phone

Snow remains on Fremont Peak even when the trees have sprouted their spring leaves.

Index

Trailer Village 27
Twin Peaks 134

U
Upper Blue 125
Upper Juan Miller 127
Upper Tonto Creek 97
Usery Mountain Regional
    Park 89

V
Valentine Ridge 98
Virgin River 20

W
White Horse Lake 33
White Rock 149
White Spar 71
White Tank Mountains
    Regional Park 86
Wild Cow Springs 58
Willow Beach 56
Windy Hill 103
Windy Point 55
Winn 119

Y
Yavapai 71

Arizona isn't all mountains and desert—aspen trees line the Apache Railroad Trail.

About the Author

Bruce Grubbs is an avid camper, backpacker, hiker, mountain biker, paddler, and cross-country skier who has been exploring the American desert for several decades. He lives in Flagstaff, Arizona, where he flies charters and fixes computers in addition to writing and photographing the outdoors. His other books include:

Backpacker Magazine Using a GPS
Backpacking Arizona
Basic Essentials Using GPS
Best Easy Day Hikes Albuquerque
Best Easy Day Hikes Flagstaff
Best Easy Day Hikes Las Vegas
Best Easy Day Hikes Palm Springs and Coachella Valley
Best Easy Day Hikes Sedona
Best Easy Day Hikes Tucson
Best Hikes Near Las Vegas
Best Hikes Near Phoenix
Best Loop Hikes Arizona
Complete 2013 Guide to the Amazing Amazon Kindle (with Stephen Windwalker)
Creaky Knees Guide Arizona
Desert Hiking Tips
Desert Sense
Explore! Joshua Tree National Park
Explore! Shasta Country
Exploring Great Basin National Park
Exploring with GPS
FalconGuide to Saguaro National Park and the Santa Catalina Mountains
Grand Canyon Guide
Grand Canyon National Park Pocket Guide
Hiking Arizona
Hiking Arizona's Superstition and Mazatal County
Hiking Nevada
Hiking Northern Arizona
Hiking Oregon's Central Cascades
Joshua Tree National Park Pocket Guide
Mountain Biking Flagstaff and Sedona
Mountain Biking Phoenix
Mountain Biking St. George and Cedar City
Publish!

For more information, check the author's website at brucegrubbs.com.

Your next adventure begins here.